# Idaho

## OFF THE BEATEN PATH™

*Gerald Thomas*

OFF THE BEATEN PATH™ SERIES

# Idaho

OFF THE
BEATEN
PATH™

## JULIE FANSELOW

*A Voyager Book*

Old Saybrook, Connecticut

Cover map copyright © DeLorme Mapping
Illustrations by Carole Drong

Off the Beaten Path is a trademark of The Globe Pequot Press, Inc.

**Library of Congress Cataloging-in-Publication Data**

Fanselow, Julie.
    Idaho off the beaten path / by Julie Fanselow. – 1st ed.
      p. cm.
    "A Voyager book."
    Includes index
    ISBN 1-56440-637-7
    1. Idaho–Guidebooks.    I. Title.
  F744.3.F36 1995              95-10695
  917.9604'33–dc20              CIP

Manufactured in the United States of America
First Edition/Second Printing

*For Natalie, who was born to travel*

# CONTENTS

# ACKNOWLEDGMENTS

Many Idahoans too numerous to name recommended special spots throughout the Gem State for this book. My thanks to all. Special thanks also go to Dick and Rowena Mallon of Hailey, Daryl Hunt of Hansen, Mike and Betsy Bullard of Coeur d'Alene, and Georgia Smith of Boise for keeping the project moving; to Karen Fothergill, Rebecca Hom, and my other Twin Falls buddies for your friendship and faith when it mattered most; and to everyone at The Globe Pequot Press for helping this book reach its audience. Finally, I am in loving debt to my family, Bruce Whiting and Natalie Fanselow Whiting. Thank you, Bruce, for being "Super Dad" to Natalie and patient husband to me as deadline neared. And thank you, baby Natalie, for sleeping through the night and lighting up my life with your sweet smiles. May we three have many more travels together.

# INTRODUCTION

When I first moved to Idaho, I had about two weeks before I was scheduled to start my job at the newspaper in Twin Falls. What better way to spend the time, I figured, than on a quick orientation trip around my new home state? Two weeks would be plenty of time to take a drive through Idaho's mountainous midsection, followed by a beeline for the Canadian border, a detour through Montana to Salmon, and a swing through Eastern Idaho.

Or so I thought. A week or so later, I'd meandered across maybe a quarter of my intended route. As someone who had grown up on the fringes of Pennsylvania suburbia and come of age in rural Ohio, I knew more than a little bit about back roads and small towns. But I knew next to nothing about a landscape that would force me, by virtue of geography and scenery, to really slow down and savor the journey, not to mention a piece of huckleberry pie here and a buffalo burger there. Half a decade and several years of book research later, I still haven't seen all Idaho has to offer. I expect it will take a lifetime, and that's fine.

In a sense, all of Idaho could be considered off the beaten path. It's true that here—like elsewhere—interstates now cross the state from east to west. But Highway 12, the only route across North Central Idaho, didn't link Lewiston to Missoula, Montana, until 1961. The new White Bird Grade on the state's only major north-south road, Highway 95, wasn't completed until 1975. And until the early 1990s, it was nonstop cross-country from Boston to Seattle on Interstate 90—except for a lone stretch of two-lane road through the town of Wallace, Idaho.

Idaho was the last of the continental United States to be settled by whites pushing westward (although Native Americans were here 10,000 to 15,000 years ago). When pioneers pressed west on the Oregon and California trails, most kept right on going through what would become Idaho. When British fur traders staked their claims in the Northwest, they did so hundreds of miles west near the mouth of the great Columbia River. Idaho's first permanent town, Franklin, wasn't settled until 1860, and many of today's communities didn't exist at all until early in the twentieth century. A few places, like Yellow Pine and Red River Hot Springs near the Frank Church-River of No Return Wilderness Area, have yet to receive telephone service.

The state's tourism slogans of recent years tell the story, too: "Idaho: The Undiscovered America" and "Idaho Is What America Was." The state's population is swelling, most notably in the southwestern corner, where Boise—frequently touted as one of America's most desirable places to live—is giving way to a creeping urban sprawl that is home to about a third of the state's population. But no matter where you are in Idaho, you don't have to travel far to escape: Owyhee County, south of Boise, and the Central Idaho Rockies, northeast of the capital city, remain so sparsely settled they could qualify as frontier. All across Idaho residents and visitors have plenty of opportunities to get happily lost for a day, a weekend, or longer, on a seldom-traveled forest road, in an abandoned mountaintop fire tower, in a country antique store, or in a tucked-away cafe.

A few notes on how to use this book: There are seven chapters, each covering one of the tourism regions designated by the Idaho Travel Council. With roads few and far between in many areas of Idaho, it is impossible to avoid retracing a route once in a while, but I've tried to keep backtracking to a minimum. Although each chapter leads off with a general map of the region and its attractions, you will want to use a more detailed map in planning your travels. You can get a free, up-to-date highway map by calling (800) 635–7820 or by writing the Idaho Travel Council at 700 West State Street, Boise 83720. The *Idaho Atlas & Gazetteer,* published by DeLorme Mapping, P.O. Box 298, Freeport, ME 04032, is another excellent reference, as are the maps published by the various units of the U.S. Forest Service in Idaho.

It's still possible to travel 50 miles or more in Idaho without passing a gas station. And just because a town is listed on a map or road sign, that's no guarantee you'll find a filling station or other services there. So before you set out off the beaten path, make sure your vehicle is in good shape and the fuel tank is full. Carry a good full-size spare tire and jack, gasoline can, and a basic emergency kit including flashers. A shovel and ax can also come in handy on unpaved back roads, the former in case you encounter a snow drift, the latter in the event a tree has fallen in your path. (Both these things happen not infrequently on Forest Service roads in Idaho's high country, even in the dead of summer.) Most of the places mentioned in this book are accessible using any two-wheel drive vehicle in good condition, but a few are unsuitable for large RVs or vehicles towing trailers. When in doubt, inquire locally before setting off on an unfamiliar route.

I've tried to list prices for most attractions, but bear in mind these are subject to change. Use the prices as a guideline, and call ahead for updates or more information. Finally, it should be noted that Idaho has more federally designated wilderness lands—nearly four million acres—than any other state in the lower forty-eight, with an additional nine million acres of roadless public land. Much of Idaho is, therefore, accessible only by boat, on horseback, on foot, or by chartered plane flown into a backcountry airstrip. For more information about exploring Idaho's wilderness areas, contact the Idaho Outfitters and Guides Association, P.O. Box 95, Boise 83701. The phone number is (208) 342–1919.

It is my hope that *Idaho Off the Beaten Path* will inspire you to hit the open road and discover this great state. Whether you seek an unusual family vacation destination, a romantic weekend rendezvous, or a fun one-day getaway; whether you desire mountain peaks, high desert stillness, or crystalline lakes, Idaho awaits your exploration. If, in your own travels, you come across changes in the information listed here or other places that might be mentioned in a future edition of this book, drop me a line in care of The Globe Pequot Press, P.O. Box 833, Old Saybrook, Connecticut 06475-0833. Thanks—and happy travels!

# NORTHERN IDAHO

2
1
Bonners Ferry

9  8

3
4 5 6
• Sandpoint

LAKES
AND FORESTS

7

13

10
11  16  14
12  • Coeur d'Alene
17 15  18 / 19  • Kellogg
THE COEUR D'ALENES  20  21 22  23
24
25

26
27

SILVER AND
GARNETS

28 29

1. Moyie River Bridge
2. Deer Ridge Lookout Tower
3. Schweitzer Mountain Resort
4. From Sea to Si Imports
5. Panida Theater
6. Vintage Wheel Museum
7. Clark Fork Field Campus
8. Priest Lake
9. Hill's Resort
10. Chef in the Forest
11. Vintage Guitars
12. Q'Emilin Park
13. Farragut State Park
14. Clark House
15. Floating Green
16. The Greenbriar Bed &
    Breakfast Inn

17. Berry Patch Inn
18. Old Mission State Park
19. Enaville Resort
20. Kingston 5 Ranch
21. Silver Mountain
22. Kellogg International Hostel
23. Sierra Silver Mine Tour
24. Northern Pacific Depot
    Railroad Museum
25. Oasis Rooms Bordello
    Museum
26. Knoll Hus
27. St. Maries Cafe & Bakery
28. Emerald Creek Garnet Area
29. Fossil Bowl

# Northern Idaho
## Lakes and Forests

Everywhere you look in Northern Idaho, you see either dense forests, expansive lakes, or both. This area of Idaho rests squarely within the Pacific Northwest, offering all the natural beauty and relaxed and friendly moods associated with the region.

Northern Idaho is noted most for its three large lakes—Coeur d'Alene, Pend Oreille, and Priest Lake (which actually is two lakes)—and the recreation-oriented resort towns on their shores. But the region also has dozens of smaller lakes scattered like constellations across the forests, and even the big, best-known lakes have their hidden bays, which are little used and ready for exploration. Rivers also run through this country; their Indian names music to the ears, their wild rapids and placid pools pure tonic for the soul. There's the Kootenai, the Spokane, the Pend Oreille, and the Coeur d'Alene. Others—like Priest River and the St. Maries—reflect the Catholic heritage of the Jesuits who came to give the local Native Americans the "medicine" of their Mass.

Two of these rivers—the Kootenai and the Moyie—meet at Bonners Ferry, the seat of Boundary County, Idaho's northernmost. East of town under a bridge spanning U.S. Highway 2, the Moyie flows through one of Idaho's most impressive canyons. The 1,223-foot-long steel truss ◈**Moyie River Bridge,** built in 1964, is the second-highest in the state, just 12 feet shy of the Perrine Bridge over the Snake River Canyon at Twin Falls. Stop at the rest area just east of the bridge for a good view of the span, or take the road to Upper and Lower Moyie Falls, two cascades that drop 100 feet and 40 feet, respectively.

The ◈**Deer Ridge Lookout Tower,** one of several current or former Idaho fire lookouts available for rent from the U.S. Forest Service, sits 24 miles northeast of Bonners Ferry. Deer Ridge and other Idaho fire lookouts and cabins are great alternatives to traditional camping, offering solitude, a roof over one's head, and unparalleled views. Deer Ridge, a 40-foot-high lookout in the Purcell Mountains, is generally available from July 1 through the end of September. Visitors are treated to a panorama featuring the Selkirk Mountains to the west and the Moyie River Valley below.

Deer Ridge is reached via the Deer Creek or Meadow Creek

roads east of Bonners Ferry, but the last mile is rough and narrow and caution is advised. Four people can stay in the tower, which rents for $20 a night, but visitors are discouraged from bringing small children because of the tower's height. For more information call (208) 267–5561 or write the Bonners Ferry Ranger District, Route 4, Box 4860, Bonners Ferry 83805. For a directory of lookouts and cabins available for rent throughout Northern Idaho and surrounding states, write the U.S. Forest Service's Northern Region Headquarters, P.O. Box 7669, Missoula, MT 59807.

If you happen to be within driving distance of Bonners Ferry at the end of September, check out the traditional **Norwegian smorgasbord** at Trinity Lutheran Church on U.S. Highway 95. This longtime event, held either the last Thursday night of each September or the first Thursday evening in October, features such delectable Scandinavian dishes as Swedish meatballs, lefse, pork roast, and pickled herring. The event typically draws a crowd of about 500 people (in a town of 2,200), and you can really fill up for about $6.00 a person. Call the church at (208) 267–2894 for this year's date. If you miss the smorgasbord, console yourself with a piece of pie from the **Panhandler Restaurant** at Kootenai and Main in downtown Bonners Ferry.

Although much smaller, Sandpoint rivals Coeur d'Alene as the most interesting town in Northern Idaho. Sandpoint's main natural attractions are Lake Pend Oreille, Idaho's largest, and ♦**Schweitzer Mountain Resort.** Schweitzer is one of the West's biggest ski areas, with 2,350 skiable acres; that and its fairly remote location help make it one of the least crowded. From the top, skiers are treated to unbeatable views of Lake Pend Oreille. At the bottom, guests can relax at the slopeside Green Gables Hotel or party in Sandpoint. Schweitzer has recently expanded its offerings to the warmer months, too. Summertime visitors can picnic atop the mountain, take a half-day or overnight guided **llama trek,** go mountain biking, or play golf. For more information on Schweitzer call (800) 831–8810.

Sandpoint is a shopping paradise, with a bevy of unique stores. Among the most interesting is ♦**From Sea to Si Imports.** Everything in the shop—sweaters, hats, home accessories, kids' clothing, pillows, purses, jewelry, and more—is from Ecuador. What's more, the prices are extremely reasonable, much less than you'd expect from a shop in a resort town. From Sea to Si is owned by Yamil and Tina Arliss. Yamil is a native of Otavalo, Ecuador, where many of that nation's great markets are located; Tina, who grew up in Lewiston, Idaho, met him while studying for a master's degree in Quito. They settled on Sandpoint as the place to open their shop, and it's a great addition to the town's eclectic, internationally flavored mix (a Scandinavian store is right next door). From Sea to Si is located at 317 North First Street. The phone number is (208) 265–1609.

Sandpoint's pride and joy is the ◆ **Panida Theater,** originally opened in 1927 and dedicated to "the people of the Panhandle of Idaho," thus the name. For years the Panida was considered one of the premiere movie palaces of the Northwest, but like many theaters, it fell on hard times in the late 1970s and early 1980s. The community rallied to buy and restore the Panida, and it now is home to a full calendar of films and performing arts. For example, one month the Panida's entertainment menu included screenings of *Jurassic Park,* a California touring company's presentation of Mozart's *Don Giovanni,* and a local theater group's production of *The Cemetery Club.* The theater is located along First Street, and patrons are welcome to bring in espresso purchased at the coffee shop next door. The Panida's box office phone number is (208) 263–9191.

Motorheads shouldn't miss a chance to explore the ◆ **Vintage Wheel Museum** at Third and Cedar streets in Sandpoint. The museum has a great collection of restored and original antique cars including a Ford Model "T" and a Stanley Steamer, along with an art gallery, a "Christmas room," and a gift shop called The Company Store. The Vintage Wheel Museum is open from 9:30 A.M. to 5:30 P.M. seven days a week year-round. A modest admission is charged. For more information call (208) 263–7173, or write The Vintage Wheel Museum, P.O. Box 993, Sandpoint 83864.

State Highway 200 runs east from Sandpoint through the communities of Hope and East Hope, both recreational gateways to the northeastern reaches of Lake Pend Oreille. Near here, in 1809, Canadian explorer David Thompson established Kullyspell House, the earliest fur trade post in the American Pacific Northwest. Nothing remains of the post, but a monument to Thompson's efforts sits along the highway at Hope.

Clark Fork, 8 miles from the Montana border on Highway 200, is home to the University of Idaho's ◆ **Clark Fork Field Campus.**

Located at the base of Antelope Mountain, the campus holds one-day workshops on topics ranging from fishing to home landscaping to environmental issues, as well as longer programs such as Elderhostel for senior citizens. Overnight accommodations for up to fifty people make Clark Fork Campus a good spot for retreats, too. More information is available by writing to P.O. Box 87, Clark Fork 83811.

Southwest of Sandpoint, Lake Pend Oreille flows into Priest River, toward a town of the same name. Head north from the town of Priest River to ❖**Priest Lake,** Northern Idaho's least-used big lake. Named for the Jesuit priests who came to Northern Idaho to spread their gospel among the Native Americans, Priest Lake is bordered to the east by the Selkirk Mountain Range, whose more than 7,000-foot peaks stand majestic against the lake's altitude of some 2,400 feet above sea level. Priest Lake is actually two lakes—the main body of water and Upper Priest Lake, which is connected to the much larger lower lake by a 2-mile-long water thoroughfare. Area marinas rent boats and other watercraft that can be used to ply the lakes and thoroughfare as well as explore island campsites dotting the water. The eastern shore is almost entirely undeveloped save for **Priest Lake State Park** and a few marinas. Nevertheless, this was where Nell Shipman—an early silent film star—had a studio during the 1920s, way up at Lionhead on the lake's northeastern tip.

The west side of Priest Lake has some commercial development, but still nothing compared to the shores of Coeur d'Alene and Pend Oreille. ❖**Hill's Resort** has been welcoming guests to Luby Bay since 1946 and has won wide acclaim for catering to families. Aside from water-based activities, Hill's is accessible to good hiking, mountain biking, volleyball, golf, tennis, hunting, cross-country skiing, and about 400 miles of groomed snowmobile trails. And then there's the food. Baby back ribs, oysters encondida, Margarita shrimp, and huckleberry pie are among the specialties, and the view of Priest Lake is a welcome side dish. Hill's has lakefront housekeeping units in four buildings, along with cabins that sleep between six and ten people. Call (208) 443–2551 for reservations or more information.

Huckleberries are plentiful in Northern Idaho, and some of the best **huckleberry patches** are located along Priest Lake. Because berries need sunlight to ripen, the best picking is often along abandoned logging roads and areas opened to sunshine by forest fires. Look for shrubs about one to five feet tall, with tiny pink or white urn-shaped flowers that blossom in June or July. The berries themselves are purplish black to wine red in color, and they generally ripen in July or August, although some berries on slopes facing north may linger as late as October.

Humans like huckleberries a lot, but so do black bears and grizzly bears. The Selkirk Mountains are one of a handful of places where the legendary grizzlies still range in the United States, so caution must always be used. (Wear bells, keep a clean camp, and retreat from the area should a bear turn up.) For a pamphlet showing prime berry picking areas and a few recipes, contact the Idaho Panhandle National Forest's Priest Lake Ranger District, HCR 5, Box 207, Priest River 83856.

## THE COEUR D'ALENES

Idaho has its share of gourmet restaurants in unlikely locations, and ◈**Chef in the Forest** certainly fits that description. Set on Hauser Lake north of the town of Post Falls, this chalet-style destination restaurant draws many patrons from eastern Washington and Montana's Flathead Valley as well as from all over Northern Idaho.

Chef in the Forest changes its menu regularly, but diners are likely to find such entrées as house specialty roast duckling with fresh brandied raspberry sauce; rack of lamb; and German sauerbraten, a Bavarian marinated pot roast complete with gingersnap sauce, potato pancakes, and braised red cabbage. Senior chef Richard Hubik (who owns Chef in the Forest with his wife, Deborah) considers himself a classical chef, steeped in traditional French and German dishes, while chef Christopher Peckham— who enjoys seafood and Mediterranean cuisine—adds an updated flair to the menu. Check out Cioppino, an award-winning dish featuring lobster, crab, scallops, and shrimp baked in an earthenware crock and served with rice pilaf and garlic bread.

Entrées at Chef in the Forest range in price from $12 to $37. A tempting variety of appetizers and desserts complements each main course, and the wine list has about fifty-five selections. To get to Chef in the Forest, watch for the sign on State Highway 53 west of Rathdrum; the restaurant is located at East 7900 Hauser Lake Road. Chef in the Forest is open for dinner only from 5:00

**Chef in the Forest**

P.M. Wednesdays through Sundays. For reservations, which are suggested, call (208) 773–3654.

Post Falls, one of Idaho's fastest-growing towns, is best known for its greyhound track, factory outlet stores, and Templin's Resort. But the town boasts another, much less heralded and obscure attraction, unless you're a musician—then chances are you've heard of ◆ **Vintage Guitars.**

James Bowers started collecting guitars in 1960 and found it "a great hobby but a lousy business." Nevertheless, he's still buying, selling, and trading all manner of stringed instruments from his unassuming shop at 316 East Fifth Avenue in Post Falls. Among his 300 instruments are a guitar once played by Elvis Presley, an acoustic guitar dating back to 1850, a Gibson "harp" guitar from 1904, and many other unusual models.

Although it's tucked away on one of Post Falls' older streets, Vintage Guitars is visible from Interstate 90, so if Bowers' reputation doesn't pull 'em in, the small neon sign in the window often will. Noted pickers who have stopped by include Leo Kottke, David Grissom, John Hartford, "and most of the guys from Asleep at the Wheel at one time or another," Bowers says. The Kentucky Headhunters once parked their tour bus right across the street and all came in together. Vintage Guitars is open from 11:00 A.M. to 7:00 P.M. Wednesday through Saturday, or by appointment. Call (208) 773–2387.

On a hot day, many Post Falls residents can be found at ◆ **Q'Emilin Park,** with its grassy lawn and beach. (Q'Emilin is a Spokane Indian term meaning "throat of the river.") Few, however, know that a magnificent canyon nearby awaits exploration. The gorge is also home to an outcropping of rocks popular with local rock climbers. To find the canyon, just stroll back beyond the boat dock and parking area.

One of Idaho's most storied state parks can be found near the town of Athol at the south end of big Lake Pend Oreille. In 1941 the U.S. Navy built the second largest naval training center in the world on this site at the foot of the Coeur d'Alene Mountains. Over fifteen months during World War II, 293,381 sailors received basic training at Farragut Naval Training Station. Following the war, the site served for a time as a college before being transformed into ◆ **Farragut State Park** in 1965. Since then the park—one of Idaho's largest—has also hosted several national Boy Scout and Girl Scout gatherings.

The park visitor center displays exhibits detailing the Navy presence at Farragut, which hasn't disappeared entirely: The military still uses 1,200-foot-deep Lake Pend Oreille as a submarine testing site. But recreation reigns at Farragut these days, with good opportunities for camping, hiking, cross-country skiing, boating, and wildlife viewing. Mountain goats patrol the steep peaks along Pend Oreille's south shore, and deer, moose, elk, and bear are also in residence. Farragut State Park is open year-round, with the usual $2.00-per-vehicle state park admission charge. For more information call (208) 683–2425, or write Farragut State Park, East 13400 Ranger Road, Athol 83801.

In the late 1980s, the F. Lewis Clark Mansion on the shores of Hayden Lake was scheduled to be burned down after years of neglect and rampant vandalism. Today, the renovated ◆ **Clark House** is one of the most elegantly appointed country inns in the Northwest.

The mansion was completed in 1910 as a summer home for Spokane flour mill magnate F. Lewis Clark and his wife, Winifred. Clark was an unusually astute businessman who, fresh out of Harvard, built the C & C Mill in Spokane, later selling it for $200,000 more than he had invested. Clark knew Spokane would grow to the east, so he turned his attention to buying land in the Idaho panhandle. Here, too, his investments proved shrewd, turning Clark into a millionaire.

The 15,000-square-foot Hayden Lake villa was considered the most grand and expensive in Idaho when it was completed in 1912. Everything about the home was opulent, from the French hand-painted wallpaper to the Czechoslovakian crystal chandeliers. Unfortunately, tragedy struck the Clarks not long after the mansion's completion when, in 1914 while wintering in California, Clark disappeared while walking on the beach in Santa Barbara. His hat was found on the beach, but a body was never recovered, and authorities never determined whether the death was an accident or a suicide. Just a few years later, Winifred Clark was forced to leave the mansion in foreclosure proceedings.

The mansion played many roles over the next decades, serving as a children's home, church retreat center, military convalescence center, and a restaurant. But the grand building had stood vacant for many years when Monty Danner purchased it in 1989. Eighteen months later, after he replaced more than 1,000 window panes, installed new heating and electrical systems, and attended to countless other details, Danner rechristened the mansion the Clark House.

The inn has five suites—some the size of midsize apartments—ranging in price from $125 to $165 per night, double occupancy (including breakfast). All have private baths with Roman tubs for two, four have their own fireplaces, and each is stocked liberally with books. Guests are free to wander the twelve acres of grounds, take in the lake views from the veranda, or soak in an enclosed hot tub.

In addition to offering the suites, Clark House frequently hosts weddings, corporate retreats and business meetings, private dinner parties, and other events for up to forty-nine people. Gourmet five-course dinners are available to guests and groups that reserve in advance.

The Clark House is geared to adults and is considered "inappropriate for children under twelve." A two-day minimum stay is required weekends from Memorial Day through Labor Day. For reservations call (800) 765–4593, or write the Clark House, East 4550 South Hayden Lake Road, Hayden Lake 83835.

In 1990, readers of Condé Nast *Traveler* magazine voted the Coeur d'Alene Resort the best resort in the continental United States. The Coeur d'Alene isn't exactly off the beaten path—its copper-topped presence dominates the city's lakefront—but it does have one amenity no other resort in the world can claim: the ❖ **Floating Green** on the resort golf course. The brainchild of resort co-owner Duane Hagadone, the green is a par 3 on the fourteenth hole. It's also a moving target, floating between 100 and 175 yards from the blue (longest) tees. The movement is controlled by a computer, with the hole's length displayed each day at the tee. More than 30,000 golfers play the course each year, and during one memorable season, 22,000 golf balls, fifty golf clubs, and two golfers landed in the lake. The golf balls are removed from the lake weekly by salvage divers, but there's no word on what happens to errant golf clubs or golfers!

The Coeur d'Alene Resort Golf Course is notable for other elements of its design, too. The links were constructed on the site of a former sawmill, and planners strove to incorporate as much of the natural environment into the course as possible. An osprey nest perches on a piling beside the thirteenth tee, and Fernan Creek and its trout spawning beds parallel the eleventh fairway. For these efforts, the course was given a special award for environmental sensitivity from the Urban Land Institute. Alas, the Coeur d'Alene golf experience doesn't come cheap. Greens fees are $125 for resort guests and $175 for everyone else. The fee includes eighteen holes, caddy service, a custom-designed golf cart for each twosome, range balls, tees, and a personalized bag tag. For more information or reservations, call (208) 667–4653.

Coeur d'Alene takes the title as Idaho's bed-and-breakfast capital, with more than a dozen establishments providing homey hospitality and new ones opening all the time. One reason for this may be Idaho's relaxed marriage laws. No waiting period is required either before or after the license is obtained, so couples from Washington, Canada, Montana, and other spots often steal away to the Gem State to seal their vows, and Coeur d'Alene is a favorite destination. There's even a **Coeur d'Alene Area Bed & Breakfast Association** available to offer information on all the local establishments, whether you are newlyweds, nearly-weds, or traveling on business. The number is (208) 664–6999.

◆ **The Greenbriar Bed & Breakfast Inn,** located close to downtown, has as its home a 1908 mansion listed on the National Register of Historic Places. Nine guest rooms feature antique furnishings and Irish down comforters. Winding mahogany staircases and arched passageways highlight the inn's common areas.

Greenbriar innkeeper Kris McIlvenna is perhaps best known for her food. The inn's nightly room rate ($45 to $65 for a room with shared bath, $60 to $95 for those with private baths) includes a three-course gourmet breakfast served at the civilized hour of 9:00 A.M. or so (although earlier meals can be arranged). The inn also offers lunch Thursdays, Fridays, and Saturdays, with elaborate and filling meals priced at about $6.00. A typical summer offering might be smoked salmon fettuccine with fresh vegetables, tomatoes, and basil in a lemon, wine, and garlic butter sauce served with a Caesar salad on the side. In colder months the special could be a hearty Czech-style goulash accompanied by rolls. High tea, served from noon to 5:30 P.M. the last three days of the week, is done in traditional English style. Far more than

11

Earl Grey and crumpets, high tea can include sandwiches, scones, soups, salads, and pastries. Reservations are requested for meals and lodging. Call (208) 667–9660 or write The Greenbriar Bed & Breakfast Inn, 315 Wallace Street, Coeur d'Alene 83814.

A ways out of town, ❖ **Berry Patch Inn** has also taken its place among North Idaho's most notable B & Bs. Surrounded by pines, this mountaintop chalet-style home is near Lake Coeur d'Alene's Cougar Bay and the headwaters of the Spokane River. As its name implies, Berry Patch Inn has its own fruit orchard. Guests can pick their own or watch deer browse among the berries, and a nightcap of berry liqueur is offered each evening. Badminton, croquet, kites, and a golf net provide warm-weather diversions, while sledding is a favorite winter pastime. Berry Patch Inn has three guest rooms, two with shared bath and one with a private bath and separate entrance. The inn is geared to adults, and smoking is prohibited inside and out. Call (208) 765–4994 for more information, or write the Berry Patch Inn, North 1150 Four Winds Road, Coeur d'Alene 83814.

The oldest standing building in Idaho is preserved handsomely at ❖ **Old Mission State Park,** accessible via exit 39 off Interstate 90. The Sacred Heart Mission was built between 1850 and 1853, the work of Coeur d'Alene Indians laboring under the supervision of Father Antonio Ravalli, a Jesuit missionary. The tribe called the mission "The House of the Great Spirit." Begin your tour by asking to see a slide presentation of the same name at the park visitor center.

The Coeur d'Alene Indians welcomed the Jesuits, for they believed the "Big Prayer" brought by the priests would give them an advantage over their enemies. There proved to be many parallels between the Native Americans and the Catholics: each had a sense of the miraculous, the crucifix and rosaries were akin to the Indians' sacred charms, the chants of the Jesuit priests weren't unlike the natives' tribal songs, and the Catholics' incense, like the Indians' sage, were both said to help carry prayers skyward.

Ravalli designed the mission in classical Roman Doric style. In addition to serving as architect, he helped adorn the insides with devotional paintings and European-style chandeliers fashioned from tin cans. Wooden ceiling panels were stained blue with huckleberry juice to resemble the sky. Incredibly, when the Coeur d'Alenes were sent to a reservation, the boundaries drawn did not include their beloved mission. A new mission was built at DeSmet, 60 miles away. But the Sacred Heart Mission (also called the Cataldo Mission) remains an important site for history buffs, as well as for Catholics and the Coeur d'Alenes who make a pilgrimage to the site each year for the Feast of the Assumption. This event, held every August 15, includes a Mass, barbecue, and Indian dancing. Other annual happenings include a Historic Skills Fair with living history demonstrations the second Sunday each July and a Mountain Man Rendezvous the third weekend of August. Old Mission State Park is open year-round, 8:00 A.M. to 6:00 P.M. July and August, 9:00 A.M. to 5:00 P.M. the rest of the year. Admission is $2.00 per vehicle. Phone (208) 682–3814 for more information.

## SILVER AND GARNETS

For more than a century, Idaho's Silver Valley—also known as the Coeur d'Alene Mining District—was the undisputed world leader in silver, lead, and zinc production. By 1985, a hundred years after mining began, the region had produced one billion ounces of silver, and the total value of wealth coaxed from the mines had topped $5 billion. Mining has fallen on hard times in recent years, with foreign competition forcing prices down below the North Idaho mines' cost of production. These days, like many Western areas formerly dependent on natural resources, the Silver Valley is looking to recreation and tourism to rebuild its economy. The region's location along Interstate 90 has proven a blessing, with many attractions visible from the freeway, but a few places require a detour from the four-lane.

The ◆**Enaville Resort** is one such spot. Dining in this restaurant is kind of like eating at a flea market. The walls are covered with collectors' plates, NASA memorabilia, and black velvet paintings, and patrons sit at extra-rustic furniture amid bulbous tree burls.

The decor leaves a bit to be desired, frankly, but the food keeps people coming back. The special here is Rocky Mountain Oysters. ("Make sure we have them. Sometimes the bulls don't cooperate," the menu cautions.) A full portion served with bread, soup or salad bar, and choice of potatoes costs $7.95, and a side order goes for $4.95. Other options include steaks priced from $7.95 to

$29.95 for the Sweetheart Steak, which is big enough for two; a good selection of seafood; chicken-fried steak; and buffalo burgers. A smorgasbord of salmon, cod, oysters, shrimp, barbecued chicken and ribs, and sautéed mushrooms is available Fridays from 5:00 to 9:00 P.M.

For much of its 115-year history, Enaville Resort has also been known as "The Snake Pit." Ask five people why, and you'll likely get five different answers. One popular tale recalls when water snakes used to inhabit the area around the outdoor privies used before indoor plumbing came along. Patrons occasionally caught the snakes, put them in a container, and brought them inside. The business also served as a way station for railroaders, miners, and loggers. In addition to food, they sometimes sought female companionship, and the women available at the roadhouse were supposedly called "snakes." The Enaville Resort is open daily for breakfast, lunch, and dinner. It's located one and a half miles from exit 43 off of Interstate 90, up the Coeur d'Alene River Road. For more information phone (208) 682–3453.

Nearby, the ◆ **Kingston 5 Ranch** may sound like a place to join the cattle drive, but it's actually a classy country-style bed and breakfast. Travelers have a choice of three rooms: the romantic Rose Room, a master suite with lace, crystal, and a private, jetted bathtub; Ginny's Attic Room, with antique furnishings and a reading nook; and Desiderata, geared to single guests with its twin bed, hardwood floors, and handmade rugs. Breakfast at Kingston 5 might include Belgian waffles with berries from the backyard patch, fresh homemade breads, and country-style meats, eggs, and potatoes. The ranch name isn't a total misnomer: Guests can do some horseback riding, and hosts Walt and Pat Gentry raise their own beef. For room rates or more information, call (208) 682–4862, or write Kingston 5 Ranch, 42297 Silver Valley Road, Kingston 83839.

Sitting atop the old, mostly dormant Bunker Hill Mine in Kellogg, ◆ **Silver Mountain** resort has made a name for itself with the world's longest single-stage people-carrying gondola. Each car transports eight people on a nineteen-minute, 3-mile ride covering 3,400 vertical feet. The gondola runs in the summer as well as in the winter. After reaching the top, many warm-weather riders like to either hike or bike down the mountain on trails ranging from 2 to 22 miles long. Skiers have their choice of fifty runs covering 1,500 acres. For more information on Silver Mountain, call (208) 783–1111.

Kellogg has one of only two American Youth Hostel properties in Idaho. (The other is in Gooding, in the state's South Central region.) ◆ **Kellogg International Hostel** offers bargain stay-and-ski packages; for example, adults can ski three days at Silver Mountain and stay three nights at the hostel for just $80 total. Kids' rates are even cheaper. The hostel's rooms sleep up to six people, and guests may fix themselves a free pancake breakfast each morning. Phone (208) 783–4171 for more details, or write Kellogg International Hostel, 834 West McKinley, Kellogg 83837.

Wallace, Kellogg's neighbor to the east, is mining its glory days with a wide selection of museums and other attractions. The ◆ **Sierra Silver Mine Tour** is billed as the only one of its kind in the Northwest. Visitors ride a San Francisco–style streetcar to the mine portal, where hard hats are issued for the trip underground. Once in the mine, participants learn about and see the equipment and techniques used to mine silver ore. Although billed as a family tour, children under four years old aren't permitted. (Guess no one makes hard hats that small.) But for everyone else, the one-hour tours leave every thirty minutes from 420 Fifth Street in Wallace. Tours are given from 9:00 A.M. to 4:00 P.M. mid-May through mid-October, except during July and August, when trips leave until 6:00 P.M. For more information call (208) 752–5151, or write Sierra Silver Mine Tour Inc., P.O. Box 712, Wallace 83873.

Train fans will enjoy a stop at the ◆ **Northern Pacific Depot Railroad Museum** at 219 Sixth Street in Wallace. The last train ran out of the Wallace depot in 1980; since then, the facility has been renovated to tell all about the Northern Pacific, which at one time boasted "2,000 miles of startling beauty." There is an extensive collection of Northern Pacific memorabilia, even a quilt bearing the railway's famous red-and-black symbol.

The chateau-style Wallace depot has a fascinating history all its own. Built in 1901 with 15,000 bricks salvaged from what was to be a grand hotel in Tacoma, Washington, the station was visited two years later by then-President Theodore Roosevelt. It has also survived a string of near-disasters: a 1906 flood, a 1910 fire that burned half of Wallace, and a 1914 runaway train that crashed only a few feet from the depot. The Northern Pacific Depot Rail-

**Northern Pacific Depot Railroad Museum**

road Museum is open daily from 9:00 A.M. to 7:00 P.M. May through October; 9:00 A.M. to 5:00 P.M. Monday through Friday during April and November; and 10:00 A.M. to 3:00 P.M. Tuesday through Saturday the rest of the year. Call (208) 752–0111 for more information.

Across a parking lot from the depot, the ◆Oasis Rooms Bordello Museum chronicles another formerly important Wallace industry, one that thrived until at least 1988. That's when the Oasis Rooms' last occupants vacated the premises, apparently in a hurry, because they left behind a variety of clothing, makeup, and perfume. The Oasis Rooms were hardly unique; at one time, five brothels stood along Wallace's main street. But this is a most unusual museum. Guided tours are available. The Oasis Rooms are at 605 Cedar Street; call (208) 753–0801 or (208) 752–3721.

Sweet's Cafe & Lounge at 310 Sixth Street has what is likely the world's second-largest collection of "bottle cars"—whiskey bottles cleverly disguised as cars and other vehicles. Cafe owner Howard "Punky" Rullman started collecting the cars thirty-seven years ago. He now has three dozen, and he's only seen one place with more, a casino in Wells, Nevada. Among those displayed are a 1909 Stanley Steamer, a 1934 Deusenberg, a Bulldog fire truck with ladders that lift up, and a 1931 Ford police paddy wagon. Sweet's also has a good collection of historic mining-era photos, along with basic American pub grub.

Photos from the past are also prominently displayed at The Beale House Bed and Breakfast, located four blocks from downtown in one of Wallace's most prominent old buildings. Hosts Jim and Linda See have collected pictures from their home's past owners, as well as from the University of Idaho's Barnard-Stockbridge Photographic Collection. Beale House has five guest rooms, one with a fireplace, another with a balcony, another with two full walls of windows. Room rates start at $75, including breakfast. Children and pets should stay with grandma. For more information call (208) 752–7151, or write The Beale House, 107 Cedar Street, Wallace 83873.

If the shopping mood strikes, head over to Silver Capital Arts at 524 Bank Street. The Queen Anne-style Wallace & Bender Building, where the shop is housed, is itself worth a look; it was among the first and largest structures built after an 1890 fire that destroyed most of Wallace's business district. Inside, Carla and

Norm Radford display and sell collectible minerals and fossils, antiques, Idaho-made silver and gold jewelry, mining souvenirs, and more. Still more mining memorabilia is on display at the **Wallace District Mining Museum** at 509 Bank Street. Along with photos, paintings, and video presentations, the museum is home to the world's largest silver dollar, three feet in diameter and weighing 150 pounds.

From Wallace backtrack along Interstate 90 to State Highway 3, the **White Pine Scenic Byway.** This route leads through country criss-crossed by the St. Joe and St. Maries rivers. The St. Joe in particular is interesting; at about 2,200 feet above sea level, it is reportedly the highest navigable river in the world. These days it's also gaining renown for its fly-fishing and challenging rapids.

Hearty Scandinavian hospitality is the specialty at ◆**Knoll Hus,** a bed and breakfast west of St. Maries overlooking Round Lake. Guests stay in a cottage about 400 feet from the home of hosts Gene and Vicki Hedlund, who provide everything from a canoe and sandy beach to two mountain bikes. Vicki brings a Swedish-style breakfast to the cottage each morning, and dinners are also available by prior arrangement. Knoll Hus can sleep up to four people; the rate for lodging and breakfast is $85 per night for two, with additional people $10 apiece extra. For more information or reservations write Knoll Hus, P.O. Box 572, St. Maries 83861, or call (208) 245–4137.

In St. Maries proper, you'll find many of the locals eating at ◆**St. Maries Cafe & Bakery.** This bright, bustling spot is popular with loggers and hunters and has a menu that reflects the geographic and economic heritage of its hometown; for example, lunch fare includes Two Rivers Chili, served in a sourdough tureen for $3.95, or a B.L.T. (Basic Logger Type), featuring bacon, lettuce, tomato, and Swiss cheese on wheat bread for $5.20. The lumber theme is carried out at breakfast, too, with The Woodsman, a breakfast sandwich on fresh deli bread for $3.75, and The Log Jam, an omelette "with everything but the kitchen sink" for $5.75. Dinners include a Stir Crazy Stir Fry for $6.25, chicken pot pie for $6.25, and chicken-fried steak for $7.25. The cafe is at 813 Main Street in St. Maries. (By the way, the town's name is pronounced "St. Mary's.") Hours are 4:00 A.M. to 9:00 P.M. weekdays and 5:00 A.M. to 9:00 P.M. weekends. Call (208) 245–5839 for more information.

Southeast of St. Maries on State Highway 3, look for two great places to have fun and maybe pick up some unique Idaho souvenirs (if you don't mind getting your hands dirty). The star garnet is found only two places in the world, Idaho and India. And in Idaho, the best place to dig for these dark beauties is the ❖ **Emerald Creek Garnet Area** 6 miles west of Clarkia on Forest Road 447. Star garnets are so named because they have rays that seem to dance across the gem's purple- or plum-colored surface. There are usually four rays, but some gems—the most valuable kind—have six. In ancient times, people believed garnets conferred a sense of calm and protection from wounds.

Garnets are typically found in alluvial deposits of gravel or sand just above bedrock, anywhere from 1 to 10 feet underground. The deposits along the East Fork of Emerald Creek are particularly rich, and visitors are invited to dig for fun and profit. First, however, a permit must be obtained at the A-frame building on the site. Permits are good for one day, and the cost is $10.00 for adults and $5.00 for children fourteen and under.

The digging areas are open from 8:00 A.M. to 5:00 P.M. daily Memorial Day weekend through Labor Day, and a Forest Service campground is situated nearby. People planning to dig should bring the following: rubber boots, waders, or old tennis shoes; a change of clothes; a standard shovel; a bucket for bailing water; a container for holding garnets; and a screen box with quarter-inch wire mesh for washing gravel. Motorized equipment is not allowed at the site. For more information call the Idaho Panhandle National Forest's St. Maries office at (208) 245–2531.

Also near Clarkia is the locally famous ❖ **Fossil Bowl,** just south of town. The Fossil Bowl was first and foremost a motorcycle racing track, but when owner Francis Kienbaum was bulldozing a new turn on the track in 1971, he unearthed a prime fossil area with a world-class stash of fifteen-million-year-old leaves, as well as a few fossilized insects, fish, and flowers. For $5.00 per person (no charge for small children), anyone can dig at the site. The fossils are found by chopping blocks from the soft clay hillside, then prying apart the layers with a knife. Some undisturbed layers that have yet to be exposed to the elements can yield magnificent leaves in their original dark green or red—until the air turns them black, usually within a minute.

The Fossil Bowl still hosts motorcycle races on Sundays mid-April through October, and anyone visiting on those days will get double for their entertainment dollar. The original fossil site is right by the racetrack, making for some dusty digging on race days, but another site farther from the commotion is now available as well. Digging is permitted year-round, but the Kienbaums suggest you call first to check on hours.

Visitors may also be interested in the Fossil Bowl's antiques collection, which includes century-old woodworking machinery. Although it's situated on Highway 3, the Fossil Bowl's legal address is 85th and Plum—"85 miles out in the sticks and Plum the hell away from everything," Francis's son, Kenneth, explains. For more information call (208) 245–3608.

# NORTH CENTRAL IDAHO

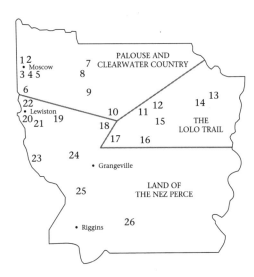

PALOUSE AND
CLEARWATER COUNTRY

THE
LOLO TRAIL

LAND OF
THE NEZ PERCE

- Moscow
- Lewiston
- Grangeville
- Riggins

1. Shattuck Arboretum
2. Lionel Hampton/Chevron Jazz Festival
3. Appaloosa Museum and Heritage Center
4. Cafe Spudnik
5. The Cottage Bed & Breakfast
6. Maiden America
7. Huckleberry Heaven Lodge
8. Elk Creek Falls
9. Dworshak Dam
10. Weippe Pizza
11. Lolo Motorway
12. Castle Butte Lookout
13. DeVoto Memorial Cedar Grove
14. Lochsa Lodge
15. Lochsa Historical Ranger Station
16. Three Rivers Resort
17. Hummingbird Haven
18. Heart of the Monster
19. Spalding Site
20. Morgan's Alley
21. Luna House Museum
22. Spiral Highway
23. Hells Canyon
24. Priory of St. Gertrude
25. White Bird Grade
26. Shepp Ranch

# NORTH CENTRAL IDAHO

## PALOUSE AND CLEARWATER COUNTRY

North Central Idaho is a land of contrast, and nowhere is this fact more visible than in Latah and Clearwater Counties, where rolling farmlands seamlessly give way to dense forests. This is the Palouse, a rich agricultural region that spills across the Idaho-Washington border.

Moscow is the heart of the Palouse and a good place to start a tour of the area. This is the home of the University of Idaho, which is blessed with a beautiful campus that includes the nineteen-acre ◆ **Shattuck Arboretum,** one of the oldest university arboretums in the western United States. Planted from 1910 to 1917, the arboretum is a pleasant place for a stroll amid native Idaho trees, as well as those introduced from other regions. Just across Nez Perce Drive from Shattuck Arboretum, the sixty-three-acre **University of Idaho Arboretum and Botanical Garden** was planted during the 1980s. It showcases trees and shrubs from around the world grouped by their geographical origin. For self-guiding brochures to both arboretums, visit the campus information center on Pullman Road (State Highway 8) and Line Street. Guided tours may be arranged by calling (208) 885–6250.

The University of Idaho is also the setting for the ◆ **Lionel Hampton/Chevron Jazz Festival,** one of the premier events of its kind. Held the last weekend each February in the university's Kibbie Dome, the festival has featured Dizzy Gillespie, Ella Fitzgerald, the Marsalis brothers, Al Jarreau, Dianne Reeves, Lou Rawls, Herbie Mann, and dozens of other top jazz stars. Leonard Feather, jazz critic for the *Los Angeles Times,* has called it "the number one jazz festival in the world." The festival also serves as a workshop for thousands of music students who travel to Moscow to play with the pros. For ticket and schedule information, call (800) 345–7402.

Idaho's state horse, the Appaloosa, is best known by the spots on its rump. The Appaloosa got its name from the Nez Perce Indians who raised it in the Palouse country of North Central Idaho and Eastern Washington. Learn everything you ever wanted to know about Appaloosas and more at the ◆ **Appaloosa Museum and Heritage Center** in Moscow. Exhibits recount the evolution of the Appaloosa, historical aspects of the breed, and its importance to the Nez Perce Indians. The museum is on Moscow's western edge at 5070 Highway 8 West, and it's open from 8:00 A.M. to 5:00 P.M. weekdays year-round and from 9:00 A.M. to 3:00 P.M. Saturdays June through September. Admission is free. Call (208) 882–5578 for more information.

◆ **Cafe Spudnik** is considered the place to eat in Moscow, with New American cuisine featuring fresh ingredients. Spudnik was one of only twenty restaurants—just two of them in the Northwest; the other was Fullers in Seattle—showcased on the public television series *Pierre Franey's Cooking in America*. Owner Denver Burtenshaw describes his restaurant as postindustrial modern yet comfortable. The decor blends black-and-white tiled floors with a stainless steel bar, and the atmosphere is akin to that you'd find in cities much bigger than this little college town.

Italian gourmet pizzas are one big draw—you can get them with such creative toppings as artichoke hearts, roasted garlic, fennel sausage, goat cheese, pesto, or prosciutto. The rest of the menu changes weekly, but entrées might include such fare as ginger tuna, steak Bordeaux, Thai chicken, and five-cheese lasagna. If none of the featured entrées strikes your fancy, chef Steve Gray will whip up something else to your liking. Cafe Spudnik is open for lunch from 11:30 A.M. to 2:30 P.M. Tuesday through Friday and for dinner from 5:30 P.M. Monday through Saturday. The restaurant is at 215 South Main Street, and the phone number is (208) 882–9257.

For accommodations in a country setting that's within walking distance of downtown Moscow, check into ◆ **The Cottage Bed & Breakfast.** Nestled in the town's Fort Russell area (named for a stockade that protected the town during the Nez Perce War), The Cottage is located behind one of the city's oldest homes. Proprietress Jean Keating has assembled a blend of country and Victorian furnishings, including a ninety-year-old wicker settee, an oversized bed, and weathered Adirondack chairs on a private wooden deck. Extra touches outdoors include a vintage birdhouse collection, flowers, a herb garden, and a big yard that was once part of a dairy farm.

At breakfast Keating—who has twenty-five years of experience as a caterer—serves a hearty meal featuring such fare as apple-stuffed French toast, homestyle sausage, herbal tea, and a frothy fruit drink. The Cottage is suitable for two people and rents for $75 per night. For more information call (208) 882–0778, or write The Cottage Bed and Breakfast, 318 North Haynes, Moscow 83843.

A short detour south of Moscow on Highway 95 leads to Genesee, a small town with a special little shop that draws customers from all over the Palouse and beyond. ◆ **Maiden America** is primarily "a floral studio," where proprietress Ellen Vieth creates art out of fresh and dried flowers; but it's also a gift shop full of unusual cards, toys, antiques, gardening gear, and so on. An adjacent tea room is the perfect setting for conversation over coffee or an Italian soda. Maiden America is at 134 Walnut Avenue in Genesee, and the phone number is (208) 285–1113.

Elk River, at the tail end of State Highway 8 east of Moscow, serves as the north gateway to Dworshak Reservoir, but this recreation-minded town of about 200 also has a few attractions all its own. ◆ **Huckleberry Heaven Lodge** rents cabins, condos, and RV spaces, along with snowmobiles, all-terrain vehicles, boats, skis, and fishing poles—just about any gear or guide folks might need to take advantage of nearby Elk Creek Reservoir and the surrounding country. Lodging options range from $18 per person per night in the inn to $70 for a loft room with fireplace to $110 for a three-bedroom condo. There's also a restaurant that serves—what else?—huckleberry pancakes each morning. For reservations or more information call (208) 826–3405.

Before you leave Elk River, take a walk around town. It's the kind of place where every family has its members' names posted on the welcome sign. There's also a handsome old schoolhouse built in 1912, perched on a hill overlooking the town. It's no longer used, but a nearby church built the same year is still in operation. For a more vigorous workout, consider a hike up 5,824-foot Elk Butte, where a panoramic view awaits all who make it to the top.

Several other natural attractions are within easy drives of Elk River. Just west of town, ◆ **Elk Creek Falls**—actually three separate falls—are reached via a set of short trails that run along what was once the old route to Orofino. If you have time to visit only one of the cascades, make it Middle Falls, at 90 feet the highest of the three. Along the way, hikers pass the site of Elk Creek Falls School, which operated between 1910 and 1930. The forest has reclaimed the building, but its gateposts still stand.

Some of Idaho's oldest and tallest trees may be seen north of

Elk River. A **Giant Western Red Cedar** estimated at more than 3,000 years old is accessed via Forest Road 4764, a branch off Road 382. At 177 feet tall and 18 feet in diameter, this is the largest tree in Idaho. Not far away, following Forest Roads 382 and 1969, is the **Old Growth Cedar Grove.** The eighty-acre stand is one of the few remaining old-growth cedar groves in Idaho, with trees estimated to be at least 500 years old.

The Dent Road leads from Elk River to Dworshak Dam and Reservoir. ✦**Dworshak Dam** is notable because at 717 feet tall, it's the highest straight-axis, concrete gravity dam in the Western world and the largest ever built by the U.S. Army Corps of Engineers. A visitor center overlooking the dam is open daily from 10:00 A.M. to 6:00 P.M. Memorial Day weekend through Labor Day, and 8:00 A.M. to 4:00 P.M. the rest of the year.

Nearby **Dworshak National Fish Hatchery** also deals in superlatives as one of the world's largest sources of steelhead trout. About three million steelhead trout, between one million and two million rainbow trout, and one million chinook salmon find their way from Dworshak into Western waters each year. The salmon are raised to help make up for the depletion in natural stocks caused by dams on the Snake and Columbia rivers. Visitors may tour the hatchery with the help of a self-guiding map from 7:30 A.M. to 4:00 P.M. each day.

Dworshak Dam backs up the North Fork of the Clearwater River into a 53-mile-long reservoir. Among the recreation opportunities on the lake and its shores are about eighty primitive camping areas, known as minicamps, that are accessible by boat only. Each minicamp is outfitted with a grill, picnic table, tent pad, and access to a chemical restroom. In recent years the campsites have frequently been rendered inaccessible because of drawdowns aimed to help migrating salmon, but Northwest water policy is evolving and the situation may change. For information on the minicamps or water levels, call (208) 476–1255. More traditional camping is available at Dworshak State Park.

Highway 12 west and southeast of Orofino is known as the **Clearwater Canyons Scenic Byway,** and it's here where the velvety brown hillsides of the Inland Northwest meet the mountains and forests of the Rockies, sometimes intercepted by vast plateaus and prairies. Take State Highway 11 east of Greer for a backroads adventure across this changing landscape.

From Greer the highway climbs a dizzying grade onto the Weippe Prairie. Weippe, a town of about 500 people, has one of Idaho's best pizza parlors. ◆**Weippe Pizza** specializes in some unusual combinations with such toppings as German sausage, jalapeño peppers, and sauerkraut. Pizza tops the menu, but soup, sandwiches, and salads are all available, too. The restaurant is open for lunch and dinner Wednesday through Sunday.

Weippe is one approach to the Lolo Trail, the famous path trod first by Indians and later by Lewis and Clark on their trek across the continent. It was just outside Weippe, in fact, that the Corps of Discovery (as President Thomas Jefferson dubbed the Lewis and Clark party) met the Nez Perce, who were to become indispensable to the white men's survival. Ask locally for directions onto the Lolo Motorway, described below.

# THE LOLO TRAIL

Lewis and Clark had been told the Lolo Trail crossing could be made in five days, but it took the corps twice that time, and they almost froze and starved en route. An early snow blanketed the mountains, and—with no game to be found—the men were reduced to eating horse meat and candle wax. Finally on September 20, 1805, Clark and an advance party of six other men dragged themselves out of the Bitterroot Mountains and onto the Weippe Prairie. Their route over the mountains can still be traced over the ◆**Lolo Motorway,** accessible from the west via Weippe or Kamiah, or from the east via Forest Roads 569 (Parachute Hill) or 107 north from Highway 12.

The Lolo Motorway—also known as Forest Road 500—is one of the roughest roads you'll encounter anywhere, but it's well worth the time and effort it takes to travel. The route is usually accessible only from mid-July through mid-September. Four-wheel drive isn't a must, but a vehicle with good clearance is advised (although the author has seen a Honda Civic traverse much of the road). Before setting out, stop at the Forest Service office in Kooskia or Powell or the visitor center at Lolo Pass on the Idaho-Montana border for maps and a detailed brochure on the Lolo Motorway route, as well as information on current conditions.

◆**Castle Butte Lookout,** a former working fire tower situated near the motorway, is a wonderful place to get away from

**Castle Butte Lookout**

civilization for a while. The lookout is available for rent from mid- to late summer; for information contact the Clearwater National Forest's Lochsa Ranger District Office, Route 1, Box 398, Kooskia 83539, or call (208) 926–4275.

The lookout is about 15 feet square and is perched on a stone foundation about 20 feet high. Visitors are treated to sweeping views in all directions, but especially to the south, where the Selway-Bitterroot Wilderness stretches beyond the Lochsa River and east into Montana. The river itself is barely visible thousands of feet below this ridge.

Castle Butte Lookout is furnished with a double bed, single cot, a table with two chairs, propane stove, and several chests of drawers. It's a great place to read, write, nap, and daydream. Visitors can also amuse themselves by learning to use the firefinder (a device consisting of a map and a sighting instrument used to determine the location of a forest fire), exploring the local terrain, or rummaging through artifacts left by previous lookout tenants: a copy of *The Smokechaser,* a memoir by former fire lookout Carl A. Weholt; a deck of playing cards; old magazines; a Western novel.

Several Lolo Trail landmarks are a short hike or drive from Castle Butte. To the east are the **Sinque Hole,** where Lewis and Clark camped September 17, 1805, and the **Smoking Place,** where the returning explorers stopped in June 1806 to share a pipe with their Nez Perce guides. To the west, the dry camp of September 18, 1805, was where Captain Clark moved ahead with six hunters to look for game. And from nearby Sherman Peak, the captains first glimpsed the Weippe Prairie. The corps called this spot **Spirit Revival Ridge,** realizing that their toilsome mountain travel was almost behind them.

Highway 12, the road the explorers' route paralleled, has many interesting sights of its own. Up near Lolo Pass, the **Packer Meadows** area is especially beautiful in early June when the purple camas are in bloom. Packer Meadows is also an excellent spot for cross-country skiing.

The picnic area near milepost 165 on Highway 12 is known as the ◆**DeVoto Memorial Cedar Grove,** named in honor of Bernard DeVoto, a noted writer and historian. Western red cedars tower here over the spot DeVoto often camped at while editing the Lewis and Clark journals, well before Highway 12 was completed in 1961. DeVoto's ashes were sprinkled over the grove after his death in 1955.

Powell, a little outpost along the highway, is the last place to buy gas until Lowell, about 50 miles west, as well as the last place to rent a roof over your head for about the same distance. The ❖**Lochsa Lodge** offers cabins and motel-type rooms for about $30 to $40 a night, and a restaurant graced with a huge fireplace serves good home-cooked meals. For more information call (208) 942–3405, or write Lochsa Lodge, P.O. Box 578, Lolo, MT 59847. Lochsa Lodge is also the base for a company called **Lewis & Clark Trail Adventures,** which offers three-day, 75-mile mountain biking treks and single-day, drive-hiking tours along the Lolo Trail, as well as white-water floats on the Lochsa River. For more information on the tours, call (406) 728–7609, or write Lewis & Clark Trail Adventures, P.O. Box 9051, Missoula, MT 59801.

**Colgate Licks** and **Jerry Johnson Hot Springs,** both located near Highway 12 west of the Wendover-Whitehouse campgrounds, are among the most popular stops along Highway 12. At Colgate Licks, deer, elk, and other animals are attracted by the springs' saltiness. Take the loop trail from the parking lot to reach the springs. The Jerry Johnson site is accessed by a mile-long trail up Warm Springs Creek. The ❖**Lochsa Historical Ranger Station,** with one of the West's best collections of Forest Service memorabilia, is also worth a stop. It's located across from the Wilderness Gateway campground, among the most pleasant along Highway 12.

At Lowell, Idaho, the Lochsa and Selway rivers meet to form the Middle Fork of the Clearwater River. ❖**Three Rivers Resort** sits at this confluence. Several lodging options exist here, including Old #1, a former ranger's cabin with modern amenities including a fireplace, hot tub on the front deck, full bathroom, kitchen, and a TV with VCR. The cabin is available April through October, and nightly rates—about $93 double occupancy—include breakfast and a bottle of champagne. For more information call (208) 926–4430, or write Three Rivers Resort, HC 75 Box 61, Kooskia at Lowell 83539.

Of the 300 or so species of hummingbirds on the planet, three of them spend their springs and summers in the backyard of Don and Ruth McCombs's home about 10 miles east of Kooskia. Stop

**Three Rivers Resort**

by and you're likely to see as many as thirty of the little hummers flitting about the feeders the McCombses lovingly keep filled. The McCombses call their place ❖ **Hummingbird Haven,** and hundreds of bird fanciers stop by each year. Ruth McCombs says the birds usually show up in mid-April and fly south for the winter about September 1. The McCombses charge no admission, but they do ask visitors to call ahead at (208) 926–4527 to let them know you're coming. Look for Hummingbird Haven at milepost 84 on U.S. Highway 12.

## LAND OF THE NEZ PERCE

The Nez Perce people—or Ne-Me-Poo, as they call themselves—have played a substantial role in the history of what is now Idaho, as well as that of the United States as a whole. For decades history students have been moved by the words of Nez Perce leader Chief Joseph who, upon his tribe's capture in Montana, made his famous "I will fight no more forever . . ." speech. Those words, uttered just 42 miles short of refuge at the Canadian border, marked the end of a 1,000-mile march punctuated by the battles of the Nez Perce War.

The war was precipitated by the discovery of gold on the Nez Perce reservation, which—by the original treaty signed in 1855—included most of the tribe's traditional homeland. When the gold was found, however, the U.S. government redrew the reservation's boundaries to exclude the areas of mineral wealth. One Nez Perce leader known as Lawyer accepted the new boundaries and signed a new treaty. But other members of the tribe, led by Old Joseph, did not agree, and soon there were two bands of Nez Perce: the "treaty" and "nontreaty."

Soon after Lawyer signed the treaty in 1867, the government launched a campaign to move all Nez Perce to the new reservation. The nontreaty Nez Perce ignored the government's orders, and for a time they were able to live peaceably. But by 1877 the government was ready to force the nontreaty Nez Perce to move, and a June 14 deadline was set.

In the meantime, Young Joseph had succeeded his father. He did not wish to move, but nor did he wish to wage war, so he moved his followers toward the reservation. Before they made it, however, three young Nez Perce men—angry at the forced move and seeking revenge for the death of one of their fathers—killed four white settlers by noon on June 14. Over the next few days, other Nez Perce joined in and an additional fourteen or fifteen whites were slain. The Nez Perce War was on.

Although the Nez Perce trail crosses through several states, North Central Idaho and adjacent areas in Oregon and Washington comprise the tribe's ancestral homeland. For that reason the **Nez Perce National Historic Park** was established in the Gem State. Unlike most national park sites, however, the Nez Perce park isn't one specific place. Instead it includes thirty-eight sites scattered across this region. Two of the most interesting are located near Highway 12 on the way to Lewiston.

Just outside Kamiah, a basaltic formation known as the ◆ **Heart of the Monster** explains how the Nez Perce came to be. According to tribal legend, Coyote—a mythical figure who is much revered in Native American literature—killed a great monster near here. The Nez Perce and other tribes were created, each as parts of the monster fell to the earth. An audio station at the site retells the legend, first in the Nez Perce's native tongue, then in English. Kamiah is also the site of the annual Chief Looking Glass Days festival held each August. This traditional pow wow features descendants of Chief Looking Glass, a Nez Perce leader, participating in dancing and other cultural activities. Call (208) 935–2525 for more information.

The Nez Perce National Historic Park headquarters are at Spalding, just east of Lewiston on Highway 95. This is where Henry and Eliza Spalding established their mission to the Nez Perce in the 1830s. A Presbyterian missionary, Spalding believed it was his duty to Christianize the Indians. "What is done for the poor Indians of this Western world must be done soon," he said. "The only thing that can save them from annihilation is the introduction of civilization."

The ◆ **Spalding Site** features an excellent visitor center that catalogs the changes—both good and bad—this philosophy wrought for the Nez Perce. Exhibits include a Book of Matthew printed in the Indians' language, a case full of beautiful beadwork, and a silk ribbon and silver friendship medal presented to the Nez Perce from Lewis and Clark. Be sure to leaf through the scrapbook bearing news articles about the Nez Perce of today.

Items include everything from the latest scholarly research on Chief Joseph to a profile of a Native American rap group.

Lewiston is the largest city in North Central Idaho, and it has more than 15 miles of trails for joggers, cyclists, walkers, and strollers. Many of these paths are on the Lewiston Levee, which was constructed by the U.S. Army Corps of Engineers to protect Lewiston after the completion of Lower Granite Dam down the Snake River.

Visit the West End of Lewiston's charming downtown for one of the city's most interesting attractions. ❖**Morgan's Alley** at 301 Main Street is a collection of specialty shops, restaurants, and a banquet facility. The "alley" is actually four old buildings linked together by thirteen stairways and seventeen brick arches. The four-level complex is owned by brother and sister Richard Morgan and Gloria Nolder, whose father once had a grocery store in the westernmost structure, the Vollmer Scott Building, erected in 1905. (Scott was one of Lewiston's town fathers; other past tenants of the building have included a foundry, a house of ill repute, and a hardware store.) When Morgan and Nolder initiated their project in the 1970s, this part of Lewiston was depressed and deteriorating, but the Alley's renovation has helped the West End rebound.

Interspersed among the Alley's seventeen shops are numerous artifacts from area history. In The Holiday House downstairs, the front of the U.S. Postal Service substation came from the post office in Pomeroy, Washington, circa 1888. A bar in the London Pub, also downstairs, was originally installed in a bar at Bovill, Idaho, about 1910. An old-fashioned gas pump marks the entrance to Bojacks, a steak-and-seafood eatery and cocktail lounge. Sets of doors came from the local sheriff's office and the Lewiston National Bank. And so on. "We gathered up everything we could find from the early days of Lewiston and the surrounding areas," Nolder says. "We grew up with these things." Tours of Morgan's Alley are available; for more information call (208) 743–8593 or (208) 746–9232.

Lewiston history is also the focus at the ❖**Luna House Museum,** operated by the Nez Perce County Historical Society at Third and C streets. The museum sits on the site occupied by one of Lewiston's first buildings, the Luna House Hotel. After serving as a hotel, the building also functioned as a courthouse for a few years in the late 1880s. Today's Luna House Museum is home to a collection of Nez Perce and pioneer artifacts, along with a striking trio of paintings by Dan Piel portraying the Indian leader Chief Joseph in his youth, maturity, and old age. The Luna House Museum is open from 9:00 A.M. to 5:00 P.M. Tuesday through Saturday, and admission is free. Call (208) 743–2535 for more information.

Lewiston spends half the month of April celebrating the arrival of spring with the annual **Dogwood Festival,** named for the hundreds of dogwood trees and perennial plants that burst forth in bloom that time of year. Events typically include an invitational art show and sale at the Lewis-Clark Center for Arts & History; the Palouse Empire Dressage Show, featuring precision horseback riding; athletic competitions; food festivals; a children's parade; and a concert. The Dogwood Festival usually takes place in late April; for more information or a schedule, call (800) 933–5272 or (208) 799–2243.

For a different perspective on Lewiston and environs, check out the famous ❖**Spiral Highway** north of town. This twisting two-lane with sixty-four curves climbs 2,000 feet to the top of Lewiston Hill. It was completed in 1917 at a cost of $100,000—about twice the projected tab. Until 1979 the Spiral Highway was the only route from Lewiston to the Palouse region above. It's still open to traffic, but most motorists now use the newer four-lane section of U.S. Highway 95. Either way, stop at the overlook at the top of the hill for a great view of Lewiston, neighboring Clarkston, Washington, the confluence of the Clearwater and Snake rivers, and the rolling farmland all around.

Lewiston is also a gateway for ❖**Hells Canyon,** the deepest gorge in North America. Hells Canyon National Recreation Area straddles the Snake River south of Lewiston and includes parts of Oregon's Wallowa-Whitman National Forest and the Nez Perce and Payette National Forests of Idaho. More than thirty outfitters offer float, jet boat, or white-water trips through the canyon. For a list contact the Hells Canyon National Recreation Area headquarters in Clarkston at (509) 758–0616. Private rafters and jet-boaters may also travel the river, but a Forest Service permit is required before launching.

South of Lewiston, Highway 95 cuts across the **Nez Perce**

**Indian Reservation,** with the aforementioned National Historic Park site and the tribal headquarters at Lapwai. Just south of the reservation border near the town of Cottonwood, the ◈ **Priory of St. Gertrude** sits high on a hill overlooking the Camas Prairie. The priory is well worth a visit for its stone chapel and a most impressive museum.

St. Gertrude's Chapel was built in 1920 of blue porphyry stone quarried nearby. Each stone was individually chiseled and placed by hand, with the nuns themselves doing much of the work. The resulting Romanesque structure and its 97-foot twin towers may be seen for miles around. The tower's bells are rung daily to call the Benedictine sisters of St. Gertrude's to services, but they're also sounded at times of severe storms as a prayer for protection. The chapel's interior is equally striking, most notably the German altar at the front. Not one nail was used to make the altar; each part was mortised and glued. A self-guiding tour brochure is available inside the chapel.

St. Gertrude's Museum is also quite a sight, particularly the Rhoades Emmanuel Memorial wing added in 1988. This section houses the collection of Samuel Emmanuel, who gave the museum a treasure trove of artistic pieces ranging from Ming ceramics to a French cabinet that appeared in the 1892 World's Fair in Chicago to a Czechoslovakian chandelier with 160 crystals. This European finery may seem out of place on the prairies of Idaho, but plenty of local lore is represented, too, most notably an exhibit about the life of Polly Bemis. This fascinating Chinese woman was nineteen years old when she arrived in the Warren mining camps of Idaho, sold into slavery for a thousand pieces of gold. She wound up marrying saloonkeeper Charlie Bemis and running a boarding house.

St. Gertrude's Museum is generally open afternoons; if not, you can ask at the convent to have the door unlocked. (Appointments to tour the museum may also be made by calling 208-962–7123 or 962–3224.) The suggested donation is $3.00 for adults and $2.50 for senior citizens. Tots are free, as the sign says.

The town of Harpster, east of Grangeville on State Highway 13, serves as the gateway to another historic road way off the beaten path. The **Elk City Wagon Road** was developed in the late nineteenth century as a route to the gold mines of central

Idaho. Earlier still, the Nez Perce on their seasonal rounds used the trail as a way from the Camas Prairie to the Bitterroot Valley in Montana. The 53-mile, mostly unpaved road doesn't appear much different now than it did a hundred years ago. Today, however, drivers can expect to traverse it in four to six hours instead of the two days (in summer) or five days (in winter) it took in the old days.

The Elk City Road is generally open June through September. To find it, look for Wall Creek Road by a group of mailboxes in Harpster and head east. Make sure your vehicle is in good condition, and fuel up before you go—there are no filling stations along the way, although gas and other services are available in Elk City. The return trip from Elk City to Harpster via State Highway 14, itself quite scenic, is 50 miles and takes about an hour-and-a-half to drive. For more information on road conditions and a self-guiding brochure on the Elk City Wagon Road, stop at the Forest Service office in Grangeville or Elk City, or call (208) 983–1963 or 842–2245.

Speaking of roads, the ❖ **White Bird Grade** south of Grangeville is easily one of Idaho's most notable highway achievements. Before it was completed in 1975, it took thirteen hours to drive from Boise to Grangeville—a distance of 197 miles. The grade replaced a tortuous old road that took 14 miles to climb 2,900 feet. (An Idaho historical marker overlooking the old road notes that if all the old route's curves and switchbacks were placed together, they'd make thirty-seven complete circles.) Yet the old White Bird Road was itself an engineering marvel, built from 1915–1921 at a cost of $400,000 to replace a wagon road. The old route—the only road linking Northern Idaho to the state capital—was finally paved in 1938. In 1974, the year before its replacement opened, the grade was added to the National Register of Historic Places.

The old White Bird Road is easily seen east of the present highway, which takes just over 7 miles to climb 3,000 feet. Stop at the pullout for a sweeping view of White Bird Canyon. This was the site of the opening battle in the Nez Perce War, described earlier. As you'll recall, several young nontreaty Nez Perce seeking revenge for the death of one of their fathers and angered by their forced move to the reservation killed a number of white settlers. In response General Oliver Otis Howard dispatched ninety-nine men led by Captain David Perry to confront the Indians at the Salmon River near here. Although they were poorly armed and outnumbered by the white men, the Nez Perce successfully turned back the Army while suffering no casualties of their own. From here the tribe started the three-and-a-half month, 1,000-mile retreat that finally ended with Chief Joseph's surrender in Montana.

The small towns of Lucile and Riggins serve as outfitting stops for the Salmon River as well as for treks into **Hells Canyon National Recreation Area** and the **Hells Canyon Wilderness.** Turn west off of Highway 95 onto Forest Road 517 for the 18-mile road to Heaven's Gate. From there it's easy to see why Hells Canyon is the deepest canyon in North America, beating even the much more famous Grand Canyon. It's because the Snake River, flowing here near sea level, is bordered by the more than 9,000-foot-high Seven Devils Mountains. The average depth of Hells Canyon works out to 6,600 feet. By contrast, the Grand Canyon of the Colorado—although much longer and more expansive—is 4,000 to 5,500 feet deep from rim to river. Visit or call the U.S. Forest Service office at Riggins for maps and detailed directions into the canyon. The phone number is (208) 628–3916.

**Northwest Voyageurs,** a Lucile-based outfitter specializing in Idaho and international river trips, also leads a four-day hiking trek into the Seven Devils that can be combined with a Snake River float through Hells Canyon. Participants spend their nights at a base camp near Hanson Lake, while daylight hours may be spent in pursuits either peaceful or challenging: Photography, fly fishing, mountain climbing, and day hiking are among the offerings. The trip is only offered twice each summer. For information on dates and prices, call (800) 727–9977, or write Northwest Voyageurs, P.O. Box 373, Lucile 83542 for a brochure.

The ◆**Shepp Ranch** is located along the Salmon River about 45 miles east of Riggins. You can't drive there, but they'll either send a jet boat to pick you up or arrange a charter flight from Boise. Once at Shepp Ranch, guests enjoy boating, rafting, trail riding, fishing, and hiking. Meals served family style feature the bounty of Idaho—trout, berries, vegetables from the ranch garden, and homemade bread, pies, and cakes. For more information phone (208) 343–7729 or write Shepp Ranch, P.O. Box 5446, Boise 83705.

A spur off Highway 95 south of Riggins leads to Pollock, a small community along the Little Salmon River. Pollock is headquarters for **R & R Outdoors** which, in addition to running one-to-six-day river trips, operates a comfortable lodge with river and mountain views. R & R also conducts specialty floats and seminars on yoga, hands-on Dutch-oven cooking, gold mining, fitness and nutrition, and more. Call (800) 574–1224 or (800) 777–4676 for more information, or write R & R Outdoors, HC 2 Box 500, Pollock 83547.

# Southwestern Idaho

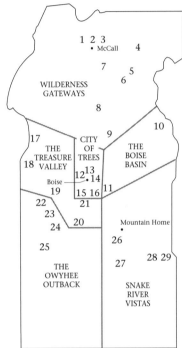

1 2 3
• McCall
4

7
5
6

WILDERNESS
GATEWAYS

8

10

17
CITY
9
THE
OF
THE
TREASURE
TREES
BOISE
18 VALLEY
BASIN

12 13
• 14
Boise
19
15 16 11

22
21
23
20
24
Mountain Home
•

25
26

THE
OWYHEE
OUTBACK
27
28 29

SNAKE
RIVER
VISTAS

1. Hotel McCall
2. McCall Brewing Company
3. McCall Winter Carnival
4. Wapiti Meadow Ranch
5. Warm Lake Lodge
6. Molly's Tubs
7. Hap and Florence Points
   Memorial Sleigh Rides
8. Payette River Bridge
9. Danskin Station
10. Sawtooth Lodge
11. Bonneville Point
12. Statue of George Washington
13. Idanha Hotel
14. Ceramica
15. Basque Museum and Cultural
    Center
16. Idaho Heritage Inn
17. Limbaugh's Farm Market
18. Fort Boise
19. Say You Say Me
20. Snake River Birds of Prey
    Conservation Area

21. World Center for Birds of Prey
22. Sandbar River House
    Restaurant
23. Givens Hot Springs
24. Owyhee County Museum
25. Idaho Hotel
26. RoseStone Inn Bed &
    Breakfast
27. Bruneau Dunes State Park
28. Three Island Crossing State
    Park
29. Carmela Winery

# Southwestern Idaho
## Wilderness Gateway

McCall has been called Idaho's most complete resort town, and with a regionally noted ski area and a spacious lake at hand, it's difficult to challenge that assertion. Many who come to enjoy these recreational riches stay at the venerable ❖**Hotel McCall** overlooking Payette Lake. Opened in 1939, the inn offers many hospitable touches including fresh flowers in each room, complimentary tea or wine each afternoon, and homemade cookies and milk each night before bedtime. A tandem bike and a recreation room complete with games and a VCR are also at its guests' disposal.

The hotel has twenty-two rooms, including one suite with a lake view. A breakfast of homemade granola, muffins, juice, and fresh fruit is served each morning at no extra charge. Rates range from $57 single or double occupancy for the lower-level rooms with shared bath to $120 for the lakeside suite. Mention you're planning an anniversary or wedding celebration, and a chilled bottle of champagne will greet your arrival. For more information or reservations call (208) 634–8105 or write Hotel McCall, 1101 North Third Street, McCall 83638.

Hotel McCall guests don't have to go far to get a good meal. The recently opened ❖**McCall Brewing Company** just up the street at 807 North Third offers some of the town's most creative cooking along with its handcrafted ales. On the food side, try a smoked salmon quesadilla, shrimp burrito, or a spicy cajun chicken sandwich. Beer varieties include Whitewater Wheat, Osprey Pale Ale, Mackinaw Red, and several others, along with seasonal specialties such as Bock, Autumn Orange Blossom Pale Ale, and Huckleberry Wheat. Relax on the upstairs, open-air deck during the summer months, or stop by for happy hour from 4:00 to 6:30 P.M. weekdays. For more information call (208) 634–2333.

The biggest winter event in North Central Idaho—and probably the entire state—is the ❖**McCall Winter Carnival.** Each year the festival draws about 100,000 people. A snow-sculpting competition is the big attraction, and there are also fireworks, a full-moon cross-country ski tour, dogsled races, wine tasting, and more. Winter Carnival takes place at the end of January each year. For information phone the McCall Chamber of Commerce at (208) 634–7631.

Southwest of New Meadows, U.S. Highway 95 leads to Cambridge, another major gateway into the Hells Canyon region (and the only canyon motor-access route generally open year-round). From Cambridge, State Highway 71 crosses into Oregon at Brownlee Dam and back into the Gem State at Oxbow Dam. From Oxbow Dam, the **Hells Canyon Scenic Byway**—an Idaho Power–owned road open to the public—runs north to its terminus at Hells Canyon Dam. There's some fine camping along the reservoirs behind these dams, even if you must negotiate the utility company's byzantine phone system to secure a spot in advance. Reservations for the spring, summer, and fall seasons are generally taken starting in mid-January. Call (800) 422–3143 for information.

Weiser, also on Highway 95 just across the Snake River from Oregon, was where Hall of Fame pitcher Walter Johnson got his start in pro baseball, hurling seventy-seven consecutive scoreless innings for the Weiser Kids of the Interstate League. These days Weiser is best known as site of the annual **National Old-Time Fiddlers Contest.** As much a family reunion as a competition, the fiddle fests have been going on in Weiser since 1914. The town became host to the Northwest Mountain Fiddlers Contest in 1953, and the national championship was inaugurated in 1963, Idaho's territorial centennial. The contest is held in late June. For this year's dates or more information, call (208) 549–0450.

The areas east of McCall and Cascade include some of Idaho's most cherished yet accessible backcountry destinations, including Warm Lake and Yellow Pine. From either spot, or points between, it's just miles to the **Frank Church-River of No Return Wilderness Area**—the largest in the continental United States. The road from McCall to Yellow Pine, Forest Road 48, is a rough but scenic route passable by any vehicle in good condition driven by a motorist using care. The road traverses huge boulder fields and immense rock outcroppings, along with areas where extensive wildfire damage is visible; this region is among those most heavily damaged by forest fires in recent years.

A few spots along the way are worth a note. The **Duck Lake Trail,** just 1 mile long, is among the easier high-country paths you'll find in these rugged parts. It's not far east of Lick Creek Summit, and the trailhead is well signed. The **Secesh to Loon Lake Trail,** part of the Idaho Centennial Trail, also takes off from Forest Road 48 across from the Forest Service's Ponderosa campground. And near the junction of Road 48 and the Salmon River Road (Forest Road 674), there's an exhibit explaining the history of the Chinese miners who toiled in the area a century ago. From 1870 through 1900, in fact, the Chinese miners had a three-to-one majority among prospectors working the Warren mining district.

Yellow Pine, with a year-round population of fifty-four, is surprisingly bustling despite its remote location. Yellow Pine folks also have a nifty sense of humor: Witness the UNIVERSITY OF YELLOW PINE sign on the town's one-room schoolhouse. You can get local information, rent videos, and buy everything from gas to diapers at Parks' **Yellow Pine Merc.** The merc's front porch serves as information central for Yellow Pine. You can read the local news (and some gossip to boot) on the bulletin board, and you might also run into Richard Alves, owner of Renegade Leather. Alves's business card reads, in part, "Wars fought, governments run, tigers tamed, bridges destroyed, uprisings quelled, revolutions started, saloons emptied" and so on. Alves boasts he can make custom gun leathers for about a third what you might pay in Boise, and they're guaranteed for life.

Most Idaho towns have an annual community bash or two, and Yellow Pine is no exception. The **Yellow Pine Harmonica Fest,** held the first full weekend of August, typically attracts between thirty and thirty-five contestants and about 1,200 spectators who crowd the tiny town for the mouth harp competition and other musical events, as well as barbecues, breakfasts, community potlucks, and a street fair. If you want to attend the festival, odds are you'll be camping out. The **Yellow Pine Lodge** has the only rooms in town, and it's not that big. If you do get in, however, you'll find ultra-reasonable rooms ($25 a night double occupancy) and home-cooked meals. Innkeeper Darlene Rosenbaum will pack you a sack lunch if your plans for the day will keep you out of town over the noon hour. To reach the lodge, or anywhere else in Yellow Pine for that matter, you must call Arnold's Aviation at (208) 382–4336, and they'll patch you through on the backcountry radio. Or, write the lodge at P.O. Box 77, Yellow Pine 83677.

Nine miles south of Yellow Pine on Forest Road 413, the traveler discovers ❖**Wapiti Meadow Ranch,** the oldest dude ranch in Idaho and one of the oldest in the Northwest. Long run by Lafe and Emma Cox, the ranch is now owned by Diana Haynes, whose background in gourmet cooking and equestrian activities make her well-suited to operate this wilderness retreat. Wapiti Meadow specializes in horseback riding and fly-fishing trips into the adjacent wilderness areas; hiking and cross-country skiing are popular, too. And Wapiti Meadow is no misnomer: Guests really are likely to see plenty of elk, especially in springtime, along with deer, moose, coyotes, and maybe a black bear.

The center of the ranch is its spacious stone and pine lodge, warmly furnished with antiques and comfortable furniture, like the big leather sofa sitting before the ample hearth. Four guest cabins are outfitted with living rooms as well as sleeping quarters. Each has a woodstove (along with modern baseboard heating), and each comes graced with fresh flowers, a coffee maker, a refrigerator stocked with soft drinks, a fruit basket, and other snacks.

You might not have room for those goodies, however, once you've had your fill of Haynes's cooking. The ranch specializes in "hearty gourmet" fare, and some guests have been known to book vacations at the ranch strictly for the food. The buffet-style breakfasts include such fare as mushroom and cheddar omelettes and hot blueberry muffins. Breast of turkey on fresh croissants and homemade tomato bisque are among the luncheon selections. And dinners range from filet of beef served by candlelight to country ribs at a Western barbecue.

Wapiti Meadow offers a wide range of packages, depending on activities selected. Ranch vacations run $165 per person per day from May through October, or $60 per person per day the rest of the year. Fly-fishing trips, including all lodging, meals, guiding, instruction, and equipment, start at $1,000 per person for three nights. Chartered backcountry flights are available from Boise. For more information or reservations at Wapiti Meadow, call the backcountry radio phone at (208) 382–4336 or (208) 382–3217 from November through May.

Forest Road 413 continues south from Wapiti Meadow to Landmark, site of a Boise National Forest ranger station. From there a good paved road takes a steep and winding plunge through heavily timbered country to **Warm Lake,** a resort and summer home area.

The **❖ Warm Lake Lodge** has been catering to backcountry adventurers since 1911. In summertime fishing and hiking are big draws, while hunters pack the cabins come fall and snowmobilers and cross-country skiers arrive in winter. But there are some less typical activities here as well, including quilting workshops and wilderness weddings. Warm Lake Lodge has twelve cabins, some with cooking facilities, priced from about $50 to $90, based on double occupancy, with additional people a few extra bucks per night. (The most expensive cabin can accommodate up to ten people.) A restaurant serves such fare as Idaho trout, breast of chicken, and homemade pies, and a lounge, general store, service station, laundry, boat rentals, and RV facilities are also available. If you're an angler, make sure to ask about Tule Lake, a trophy cutthroat fishery southwest of Warm Lake. Warm Lake Lodge is open year-round. Reservations may be made by calling (208) 257–2221 or writing Warm Lake Lodge, Warm Lake 83611. If this lodge is full, the nearby North Shore Lodge has similarly priced cabins and services.

❖**Molly's Tubs,** one of several hot springs in the area, sit on the South Fork of the Salmon River just a few miles west of Warm Lake. Look for Forest Road 474 on the south side of the road, then drive 1.3 miles to a small pullout on the right-hand side. A short but somewhat steep path leads down to an array of real bathtubs, hauled to the site for your soaking pleasure. At last count there were nine collected amid the cathedral of pines. A hose has been rigged up from the spring to the tubs. The water is too hot to sit in, but a big bucket sitting nearby may be used to haul cold water from the Salmon until just the right temperature is achieved.

The Warm Lake Road winds up back in Cascade, a recreation-oriented town at the south end of Cascade Reservoir and the scenic Long Valley. Summer or winter there's lots to do here. In the colder months, check to see if the ❖**Hap and Florence Points Memorial Sleigh Rides** nearRoseberry are in operation.

The sleigh rides take place on the Points Ranch where, years ago, Hap Points started feeding the elk that came down to winter in the Goldfork River Valley. It was either that or see his cattle starve, since the elk would run the cows off and eat their hay. Hap just started setting out extra hay for the elk, and all the critters were happy.

Word soon got out that the elk were congregating on the Points Ranch, and folks came from miles around to see them feed. Unfortunately, that scared off the elk. These days, visitors can go along to feed the elk by reservation only, but that makes

**Molly's Tubs**

for a better experience. In fact the elk are so used to the horse-drawn sleds that they will come right up and eat off the hay bales on which the riders sit. This is one of only a few places in the West where it's possible to see bulls, cows, and calves all together.

The sleigh rides are now run by Vicki Eld, a neighboring rancher who helped Hap Points feed the elk; her husband, Joe; and the Points's son, Lyle, and his wife, Kathy. They all know a lot about elk and can even relate stories about individual members of the herd. The sleigh ride season varies every year, depending on when the elk appear: It begins anywhere from Thanksgiving to late January and ends as early as February and as late as April. But once it starts, it runs seven days a week until it's over. Cost is $8.00 for adults and $5.00 for children. For more information or reservations call Vicki and Joe at (208) 325–8876.

**The Creamery Bed & Breakfast** in Cascade caters to folks either passing through or vacationing in the area. This cozy spot is furnished in a blend of Early American and farm decor, with four rooms priced by the number of people: from $40 for a solo traveler to $100 for four folks sharing a room. In the evening guests can enjoy piano music and conversation in the parlor. And in the morning breakfast is served by the woodstove, with a typical repast featuring fresh fruit and breads, hot and cold cereals, yogurt, and a variety of egg and meat dishes. Call (208) 382–4621 or write The Creamery Bed & Breakfast, 314 Main Street, Cascade 83611 for information or reservations.

South of Cascade, the Payette River can't help but command the traveler's attention, with plenty of handy pullouts for fishing, picnicking, or even taking a dip on a scorching summer day. Keep the camera handy, too: The graceful yet sturdy ◆**Payette River Bridge** south of Cascade is one of Idaho's most picturesque. Hang a left at Banks for a trip into the Boise Basin, a former mining hotbed still rich in scenic wealth.

## THE BOISE BASIN

East of Banks, the two-lane Banks-Lowman Highway leads through scenic Garden Valley. This road wasn't even paved until the early 1990s, but locals now say it's the best road in Boise County. It's no slouch on scenery either; the South Fork of the Payette, which had its headwaters near Grandjean, tumbles far below the road. Incredibly, this backcountry stretch also has a gourmet restaurant. ◆ **Danskin Station,** located 10 miles east of Garden Valley on the Banks-Lowman Highway, is only open Fridays, Saturdays, and Sundays, so plan accordingly. Its building doesn't look like much, but the food draws raves. The menu changes each weekend and features such fare as steak Provençale, fresh king salmon, a chicken burrito with green salsa, and sweet and sour pork. For dessert just try and pass up choices like amaretto cheesecake or fried pecan torte. Danskin Station is open from 10:00 A.M. to 9:30 P.M., and reservations are accepted. The phone number is (208) 462–3884.

If you're in the area on a weekday and Danskin Station isn't open, the **Country Inn** at Garden City and the **Longhorn Restaurant** in Crouch are good alternatives. The latter is more off the beaten path; Crouch sits a mile from the highway, up the Middle Fork of the Payette River. The Longhorn, in business since 1947, basically looks like a glorified country-and-western road-house, but the menu is wide and the portions ample. Breakfast offerings include omelettes, biscuits and gravy, and something called a Stove Lid Sandwich—two pancakes, sausage or bacon, and one egg served sandwich style for $4.25. Lunch and dinner are heavy on the beef, with burgers weighing in at a third of a pound and roast beef on the menu Saturday nights. None of this comes as a surprise in logging country, but the Longhorn also offers several vegetarian dishes.

At Lowman, State Highway 21 treks north to Stanley (see the Central Idaho Mountains chapter) and south to Idaho City. A short spur off the northern stretch leads to Grandjean. This tiny town on the western slope of the Sawtooth Mountains is literally within the Sawtooth Wilderness Area boundaries; although designated wilderness areas don't normally have roads (much less a resort), Grandjean was grandfathered in when the boundaries were drawn, which seems appropriate since the town was named for the Boise National Forest's "grandfather," Emile Grandjean, first supervisor of the forest from 1908 to 1919.

Grandjean is home to the ◆ **Sawtooth Lodge.** More accurately, you could say the Sawtooth Lodge *is* Grandjean. The lodge serves meals from 8:00 A.M. to 8:00 P.M., with hearty mountain fare topping the bill. Log cabins sleep from two to four people at prices ranging from about $35 to $70 a night. Outdoors, guests are free to enjoy a warm mineral-water plunge pool, wildlife viewing, hiking, and fishing. RV and tent camping facilities are available, too, and it should also be noted that Grandjean makes an ideal vacation destination for folks with handicaps; one of the Sawtooth Lodge's cabins is outfitted for people with disabilities, and a mile-long nature trail is wheelchair-accessible.

Sawtooth Lodge usually opens Memorial Day and closes around mid-October. For current rates, reservations, or other information, call (208) 259–3331, 344–6685, or 344–2437. The mailing address is 1403 East Bannock, Boise 83712. Sawtooth Lodge is also home to **Sawtooth Wilderness Outfitters,** which provides horses and guides for trail rides and pack trips into the wilderness area. The outfitters' phone numbers are (208) 259–3408 summer or (208) 462–3416 winter, with a mailing address of P.O. Box 81, Garden Valley 83622.

Although not as well known as the '49ers' rush to the California gold fields or the boom in the Yukon, Idaho miners had glory days all their own. During the 1860s, in fact, more gold was mined from the mountains northeast of Boise than from all of Alaska. **Idaho City,** epicenter of this boom, was once the largest city in the Northwest. Today it's a town oriented to tourism and recreation in the neighboring Boise National Forest.

Like most mining towns, Idaho City had a reputation as a wild place to be. It's been reported that only 28 of the 200 people buried in the town's Boot Hill died a natural death. These days, however, it's much more calm—even peaceful—with a small selection of visitor services and abundant recreation nearby. The areas around Idaho City are justly famous for great hiking and cross-country skiing.

When Highway 21 intersects with Interstate 84, it's just a few miles west to Boise. First, however, you might want to head east for a few miles to see Idaho's capital city as our forebears did, from ◆**Bonneville Point.** This was the spot from which mountain men and Oregon Trail pioneers first spied the verdant Boise River valley below. Boise got its name, in fact, when a party of French trappers visited Bonneville Point in 1833. For weeks the trappers had seen nothing but lava and sagebrush. Now, far below them but less than a day's walk, they saw a verdant river valley, the streambank lined with trees. "Les bois, les bois, voyez les bois" ("The trees, the trees, look at the trees"), the trappers cried in joy. The name stuck, and to this day Boise is known as the "City of Trees."

To find Bonneville Point, take exit 64 off of Interstate 84 and follow the signs north. The Bureau of Land Management has placed an interpretive kiosk at the site, and a long stretch of wagon-wheel ruts may be seen nearby, along with a beautiful look at Boise and its foothills. "When we arrived at the top we got a grand view of the Boise River Valley," emigrant Cecilia E. M. Adams noted in her diary. The trees they saw, she added, were "the first we have seen in more than a month." Likewise, explorer John Fremont, who mapped the West, wrote of his joy in seeing the Boise River, "a beautiful rapid stream, with clear mountain water" and noted he was "delighted this afternoon to make a pleasant camp under fine old trees again."

## CITY OF TREES

Boise is one of the nation's fastest-growing cities. Nevertheless, it remains wonderfully compact, with many of its most interesting sites within walking distance downtown. Looming over all is the State Capitol, which makes a logical spot to begin explorations. Although the Capitol itself isn't "off the beaten path," its interior harbors some little-known and fascinating lore.

For example, check out the replica of the *Winged Victory of Samothrace,* a marble statue sculpted around 300 B.C. The original stands in the Louvre in Paris; in 1949 France gave a replica to each American state as a gesture of thanks following World War II, but Idaho's copy is supposedly the only one on public view in a statehouse. Then there's the one-of-a-kind ◆ **statue of George Washington** astride a horse on display just outside the attorney general's office on the second floor. The statue was created by Charles Ostner, a self-trained artist, Austrian immigrant, and Payette River ferry operator who took four years to carve the statue from a single piece of yellow pine, working by candlelight. No one is sure what the statue is worth, but the Smithsonian Institution reportedly once sought—unsuccessfully—to add the work to its collections. Ostner presented the bronzed statue to the Idaho territorial government in 1869 and it stood outside on the Capitol grounds until 1934, when, weather damaged, it was brought indoors and re-covered with gold leaf.

The case in which Washington's statue stands also sports the only Idaho state seal of original design still left in the Capitol. The original seal, updated in 1957, was created in 1891 by Emma Edwards Green, winner of a national competition and the only woman to design a state seal in America. (Green placed just her initials on her entry, fearing the design would not be chosen if officials knew it was the work of a woman.) Another Idaho first: The state elected the nation's first Jewish governor, Moses Alexander, who served from 1915 through 1919. His portrait, along with those of other past chief executives, may be seen outside the present governor's office, also on the second floor. Duck inside the governor's suite to sign the guest book and pick up a free Idaho potato pin!

Self-guided Capitol tour brochures are available in the governor's office or at the travel information booth on the statehouse's main floor. Personal tours are also available weekdays, but it's best to call (208) 334-2470 to arrange one in advance (except during the state legislative session, generally January through March, when (208) 334-2000 is the number to call).

Just a few blocks from the statehouse, Boise's storied ✦ **Idanha Hotel** continues to welcome guests at 928 Main Street. When the French chateau-style hotel opened in 1901, it was the state's first high-rise building (with five and a half stories) and the first with what was then called "an electric lift." (We now call it an elevator.) Theodore Roosevelt and Ethel Barrymore were among early patrons to sign the hotel's register.

The Idanha's old rooms might be considered a bit funky in contrast to other, newer, Boise lodgings, but the hotel offers some of the best package deals in town. One recent special included a "deluxe historic room" for two, a $40 gift certificate toward dinner at Peter Schott's Restaurant (located on the premises and generally considered one of Idaho's best), two movie passes, two-for-one drink coupons good at the hotel lounge, and continental breakfast for two, all for $83. For reservations or more information call (208) 342-3611.

**Old Boise,** the area just east of Capitol Boulevard, is chock-full of intriguing stores, restaurants, and other spots. If the creative impulse strikes, be sure to stop in at ✦ **Ceramica,** a gallery and drop-in workshop in the Pioneer Building at Sixth and Main.

Former international money trader Jennifer Sorensen had dabbled in art for years when she decided the time might be right to establish a contemporary ceramics gallery and workshop in Boise. Patrons are invited to choose a ready-to-paint piece, with selections ranging from pots and plates to piggy banks priced from $4.00 to $40.00 (including up to four colors of paint and glaze). After that, they're seated at a table, given some instruction and advice, and encouraged to let their imainations run wild.

A set-up charge of $6.50 per person is levied for the first hour and a half at the workshop. Sorensen says most people complete their painting and glazing within ninety minutes, but dawdlers can take their time at the rate of $1.00 per extra fifteen minutes. The price also includes firing, and patrons can typically pick their completed piece up the day after they begin.

Sorensen has been surprised at the varied clientele her studio attracts. One regular customer, an art major turned lawyer, says Ceramica has helped him rediscover his creative roots. The shop is also a viable first-date alternative; Sorensen says it's amazing how much you can learn about a person from the way he or she approaches art. For example, "if you get someone painting skeletons, you know there may be a problem," she notes. Ceramica operates on a no-appoitnment-necessary basis, but it can also be rented for parties and showers. (One bride-to-be had her friends paint her a unique set of not-quite-matching plates. (The workshop is open from 10:00 A.M. to 9:00 P.M. Tuesday through Thursday and 10:00 A.M. to 10:00 P.M. Friday and Saturday. Call (208) 342–3822 for more information.

Idaho has the nation's highest percentage of people hailing from Euzkadi, or the Basque homeland that straddles the border of Spain and France. Although pockets of Basque culture can be found throughout the state, Boise, by virtue of its size, is probably the state's true Basque capital. And a 1-block area of the capital's downtown is an especially rich site of Basque heritage and culture. Don't pass up a opportunity to take a stroll down Grove Street between Sixth and Capitol for a look at what could be called Boise's Basque Block.

Starting from the block's east end and moving west, the Basque Center at 601 Grove was built in the late forties as a social club and gathering place, a role it continues to play today.

The center is a popular site for wedding receptions, dinners, and dances, but it serves as an informal meeting spot, too, particularly for older Basques who enjoy drinking coffee, talking, and playing "mus," a Basque card game.

Until recently the **Cyrus Jacobs-Uberuaga House** at 607 Grove housed the Basque Museum and Cultural Center (which has since moved next door). Built in 1864, this is the oldest brick building still standing in Boise, site of the city's first indoor bathtub and the wedding of Senator William Borah. The building served as a Basque boarding house for much of the twentieth century, and the local Basque community plans to renovate it to reflect that heritage.

At 611 Grove, the ◆ **Basque Museum and Cultural Center** has many fascinating exhibits on all aspects of Basque history and culture. Here you can learn, for example, about famous people of Basque heritage, including Simon Bolivar, Francisco Goya, Balboa, and Juan de la Cosa, who served as Columbus's navigator. Another Basque mariner was responsible for guiding Magellan's ship home after the explorer was killed in the Philippines following the first circumnavigation of the globe.

Visitors discover that most Idaho Basques trace their heritage to the province of Vizcaya in the northwest section of the Basque homeland. Here, too, are history lessons about Gernika, Boise's sister city and the ancient Vizcayan capital and spiritual homeland of the Basques. It was the bombings here during the Spanish Civil War of 1936–1939 that inspired Pablo Picasso's *Guernica* painting, one of his most famous. Gernika is also home to an oak tree that symbolizes Basque liberty; a model of the tree and its surroundings sits in the museum. The Basque Museum is open from 10:00 A.M. to 4:00 P.M. Tuesday through Friday and from 11:00 A.M. to 3:00 P.M. Saturday. Suggested donation is $1.00 for adults and 50 cents for children and senior citizens. Call (208) 343–2671 for more information.

The **Fronton Building** at 619 Grove was built in 1912 and, although it has housed businesses over the years, none has ever altered the fronton, or handball court, inside. It is the largest covered court of its kind in the Northwest, and it is still used by sporting Basques today. This building also served as a boarding house for a time.

**Basque Center**

**Bar Gernika,** at the corner of Grove and Capitol, is a Basque pub and restaurant established in 1991. The menu here includes several Basque-inspired dishes such as a Solomo sandwich (marinated pork loin topped with pimentos and served on a French roll) or a cheese plate accompanied with fresh bread and grapes. Espresso and microbrews are available, too. Bar Gernika is open from 11:00 A.M. to 11:00 P.M. Monday through Thursday, 11:00 A.M. to 1:00 A.M. Friday, and noon to 1:00 A.M. Saturday. The phone number is (208) 344–2175. Although it's not on the Basque Block, diners interested in Basque cuisine may also want to try Onati at 3544 Chinden Boulevard in nearby Garden City. There, Basque chefs prepare meals of lamb, fish, steaks, shrimp, and prawns. Call (208) 343–6464 for reservations or more information.

Boise visitors seeking a bed-and-breakfast stay should consider the ◆**Idaho Heritage Inn** at 109 West Idaho, in the midst of the Warm Springs neighborhood of gracious old homes. Built in 1904 for Henry Falk, one of Boise's early merchants, the home was bought by Idaho Governor Chase Clark in 1943. Later, Clark's daughter, Bethine, and her husband, the beloved Senator Frank Church, used the home as their Idaho residence during Church's Senate tenure. The home remained in the Clark/Church family until 1987, when Tom and Phyllis Lupher bought it with an eye toward opening a bed and breakfast.

The Idaho Heritage Inn offers guests a choice of six rooms ranging in price from $59 to $89 for two. Each has a private bath, queen-size bed, and telephone, making this a good spot for business travelers. Room rates also include a breakfast featuring fresh-squeezed juice and fresh fruit in season along with an entrée: Baked German pancakes, apricot cream cheese–stuffed French toast, and apple skillet cake are among past offerings. Call (208) 342–8066 or write the Idaho Heritage Inn, 109 West Idaho, Boise 83702 for more information or reservations.

## THE TREASURE VALLEY

Picture a bright fall day. What do you think of? Piles of fat orange pumpkins? Baskets of tart, crisp apples? Roadside markets piled high with the harvest's bounty?

Southwestern Idaho is the state's fruit bowl, and a good place to get a taste of it is the Fruitland area, just over the border from

Oregon north of Interstate 84. Rush over to ◆ **Limbaugh's Farm Market** in late September or early October for some fresh apple cider. Limbaugh's, owned by distant cousins of talk radio's right-wing king, stocks Idaho gourmet food gifts, beautiful wind socks, fruit baskets, farm-fresh veggies, and a wide selection of nuts and candies. Just before Thanksgiving the market is transformed into a holiday wonderland with decorated trees and lights. Limbaugh's is located along Highway 95 north of Fruitland, and it's open seven days a week April through December. The phone number is (800) 525–1402.

The small town of Parma on U.S. Highway 20/26 is home to a replica of the Hudson's Bay Company's ◆ **Fort Boise,** built in 1834 and one of two nineteenth-century forts so named. (The town of Boise grew up around the other, a U.S. Army cavalry post erected in 1863.) The British-run Hudson's Bay Company built Fort Boise partially in retaliation for the American presence Nathaniel Wyeth had established at Fort Hall, near what is now Pocatello.

The original Fort Boise was situated on the east bank of the Snake River about 8 miles north of the mouth of the Boise River. Although it was built as a fur-trading post, Fort Boise soon switched its emphasis to serving emigrants on the Oregon Trail, and it was a most welcome sight after 300 miles of dry and dusty travel from Fort Hall. An 1845 report on the fort told of "two acres under cultivation . . . 1,991 sheep, seventy-three pigs, seventeen horses, and twenty-seven meat cattle," but the pioneers frequently depleted the fort's stores of flour, tea, coffee, and other pantry staples.

Flooding extensively damaged Fort Boise in 1853, and historians believe any attempts to rebuild it were probably thwarted by increasingly hostile relationships with the Shoshone Indians. Tensions culminated with the 1854 Ward Massacre, in which eighteen emigrants (out of a party of twenty) died; a monument marking the event may be seen in a park south of Middleton, Idaho. Hudson's Bay Company abandoned Fort Boise two years later, and the land on which it originally stood is now a state wildlife management area.

The Fort Boise Replica in Parma sits 5 miles southeast of the original fort site. In addition to the emigrant story, the Fort Boise Replica has artifacts and displays from Southwestern Idaho history. One room features a desk built in 1891 by a boy whose family was traveling to Oregon when their money ran out and they decided to stay. Another exhibit tells how Parma is the only Idaho town to have produced two Gem State governors: Clarence Baldridge, a Republican, and Ben Ross, a Democrat. Visitors may also view a video on Fort Boise history.

A statue and historical marker on the Fort Boise grounds are also worth noting. They tell of Marie Dorian, an Iowa Indian who came to the area with Wilson Price Hunt's party of Astorians in 1811. Three years later, Marie and her two children were the sole survivors of a midwinter battle with Bannock Indians at a nearby fur-trading post. They set out with two horses on a 200-mile journey through deep snow and were finally rescued by a Columbia River band of Walla Walla Indians in April.

The Fort Boise Replica is open from 1:00 to 3:00 P.M. Fridays, Saturdays, and Sundays during June, July, and August, but if you want to see it during off-hours, you can call the Parma City Hall at (208) 722–5138 to make arrangements. The park adjacent to the fort replica includes a small campground with showers and a dump station, as well as shady picnic spots, a playground, and a drive-in restaurant next door. Parma celebrates its role in pioneer history late each May with the Old Fort Boise Days celebration.

Idaho's vineyards may never become as well known as those in California's Napa Valley, but the Gem State has a growing number of wineries, with the largest concentration in the state's southwestern region. Warm days, cool nights, and rich soil make valleys along the Snake River just right for growing wine grapes. Ste. Chapelle at Sunny Slope near Caldwell is probably Idaho's best known winery, drawing many visitors for tours and its summer jazz concert series. But other local vineyards worth a visit include Pintler Cellar at 13750 Surrey Lane south of Nampa, with its panoramic view and annual Mother's Day Wine and Food Festival; Weston Winery, one of the state's oldest, at 14949 Sunny Slope Road, Caldwell; and Hells Canyon Winery, 18835 Symms Road, Caldwell. Pintler is open weekend afternoons for tours and tasting, Weston offers the same on Fridays and Saturdays, and Hells Canyon maintains its tasting room at Mussel's Fish Market, 3107 Overland in Boise.

If you're traveling along Interstate 84 when the hungries hit, you could pull off almost any exit into a wide selection of chain fast-food eateries. Or you could wander a bit farther from the freeway for the homemade fare served by Nampa's ◆ **Say You Say Me.**

This locally popular cafe is famous for its eight-egg omelettes, although owner Dayle Blamires and his staff have been known to slip in as many as a dozen eggs. At lunchtime patrons can choose from among twelve different burgers. Dinner fare includes T-bone steaks (the most expensive item on the menu at $13.50), chicken-fried steaks, and chicken fajita salad. Prices are as low as the portions are huge. Say You Say Me, located at 820 Nampa-Caldwell Boulevard, is open from 6:00 A.M. to 9:00 P.M. Monday through Saturday, and 6:00 A.M. to 3:00 P.M. Sundays. The phone number is (208) 466–2728.

The Snake River Canyon in Southwestern Idaho is home to the world's largest concentration of nesting eagles, hawks, and prairie falcons. There are two ways to discover this raptor kingdom: Tour the ◆**Snake River Birds of Prey Conservation Area** and visit the Peregrine Fund's ◆ **World Center for Birds of Prey** near Boise.

The conservation area encompasses more than 482,000 acres along 81 miles of the river, and it's best reached via the Swan Falls Road south of Kuna. The Bureau of Land Management has established an interpretive area near Swan Falls Dam, and visitors may catch a glimpse of raptors soaring through the canyon or nesting in its cracks, crevices, and ledges. Early morning and late afternoon mid-March through mid-June is the best time to visit. Bring binoculars, a bird field guide, water and food, sunscreen, a jacket, and a hat.

Because the raptors can be difficult to see from the top of the canyon, some people prefer a bottom-up view from the deck of a tour boat. **Whitewater Shop River Tours,** based in Kuna, offers a variety of excursions starting at $50 per person. Guides help participants identify bird species and locate the raptors' nesting areas. A few trips each year are accompanied by Morley Nelson, who was instrumental in establishing the Birds of Prey Conservation Area. For more information or trip reservations, call (208) 922–5285, or write Whitewater Shop River Tours, 252 North Meridian Road, Kuna 83634.

Scientists study raptors because, like humans, they are near the top of the food chain—and what happens to them could very well happen to us. Four decades ago, the peregrine falcon (for which The Peregrine Fund is named) had almost been wiped out.

Through research it was learned that falcons ate smaller birds that had in turn ingested insects exposed to DDT, and the chemical made the falcons' eggshells so thin that the baby birds could not survive.

DDT is now banned in the United States, and the peregrine falcon has made an impressive comeback on our continent. But the chemical remains legal in some other nations; that fact, coupled with other environmental woes, has endangered or threatened nearly a quarter of the world's 300 raptor species. So The Peregrine Fund continues to study birds of prey and their status as environmental indicators, and much of this work takes place at the World Center for Birds of Prey and its new Velma Morrison Interpretive Center sitting high on a windswept hill south of Boise.

Visitors to the center can walk around on their own or join a guided tour. Through films, lectures, and displays visitors learn how The Peregrine Fund breeds raptors in captivity, then sets them free in their natural habitat. The odds against survival can be high: All peregrines, whether captive-bred or born in the wild, face a 50 percent mortality rate during their first year of life. Another 20 percent die in their second year. But those who survive two years usually go on to live an average of fifteen years. At the end of each tour, visitors are often treated to a visit with a live falcon. The World Center for Birds of Prey is open from 9:00 A.M. to 5:00 P.M. Tuesday through Sunday. Take exit 50 from Interstate 84 and drive south 6 miles on South Cole Road to Flying Hawk Lane. Suggested admission is $4.00 for adults and $2.00 for children and senior citizens. Call (208) 362–8687 for more information.

## THE OWYHEE OUTBACK

Owyhee County deserves its own section in any book about Idaho's lesser-known places, simply for its sheer size and remoteness. It isn't Idaho's biggest county—Idaho County takes that honor with 8,497 square miles. But Owyhee County, tucked into the state's corner, is mostly unexplored and unknown. At 7,643 square miles, it's larger than New Jersey, but with about one-nine-hundreth the population!

Nearly half the county's population lives in the Homedale-Marsing area along the Snake River southwest of Caldwell. Lucky people, they can eat at the ◆**Sandbar River House Restaurant** anytime they want. This classy yet casual eatery in Marsing attracts people from Boise and beyond in search of some of Idaho's best dining. House specialties include prime rib (served Fridays, Saturdays, and Sundays), lamb sirloin steak, buffalo ground steak, and beef en brochette. Seafood and chicken are also on the menu, and patrons are invited to make a combo dinner by adding such side orders as shrimp scampi, fresh mushroom topping, or a rock lobster tail to their main dish. A deck beckons for guests who want to dine outside, overlooking the river. The Sandbar River House is open for lunch and dinner from 11:00 A.M. to 9:30 P.M. Tuesdays, Wednesdays, and Thursdays, and from 11:00 A.M. to 10:30 P.M. Fridays and Saturdays. Dinner only is served from noon to 8:00 P.M. Sundays, and the restaurant is closed Mondays. Call (208) 896–4124 for reservations, which are recommended.

While in Marsing, look for **Lizard Butte,** the volcanic formation looming over town. Waterfall lovers may wish to travel west of Marsing to see **Jump Creek Falls.** (Ask locally for directions.) The falls, a silver ribbon cascading into a placid pool, are part of the Bureau of Land Management's Jump Creek Special Recreation Management Area, an area of desert plateau and canyonlands west of the intersection of Highways 55 and 95.

◆ **Givens Hot Springs,** 12 miles from Marsing, got its start as a campground on the Oregon Trail. Pioneers frequently stopped here to wash their clothes; one emigrant said the water was "sufficiently hot to boil eggs." Before that, Native Americans used the area as a base camp. Milford and Martha Givens, pioneers themselves, had seen the springs on their way west. Once they got where they were going, however, they decided they liked Idaho better and came back.

The first Givens Hot Springs bathhouse was built way back in the 1890s, and a hotel stood on the grounds for a while as well. Givens Hot Springs is still a campground, with an enclosed year-round swimming pool, private baths, picnic grounds, softball and volleyball play areas, horseshoe pits, cabins, and RV camping. For more information call (208) 495–2000.

Murphy, the seat of Owyhee County, has a sense of humor. Why else would there be a lone parking meter in front of the county courthouse? This town of about fifty people is also home to the ◆ **Owyhee County Museum,** housed in a building that also includes the local library. The museum features varied displays of early county artifacts ranging from Indian tools to cowboy gear. Visitors also learn about life in the early mining towns, seen from several perspectives including that of the many Chinese miners who lived and worked in Idaho during the nineteenth century. The museum is open from 10:00 A.M. to 4:00 P.M. Wednesday through Friday year-round, as well as some summer weekends. Suggested donation is $1.00 for adults and 50 cents for children. Call (208) 495–2319 for more information or current operating hours.

If you enjoy old mining towns, don't miss Silver City. Although fairly well known, Silver, as the locals call it, is decidedly off the beaten path, an often rough and winding 23-mile drive southwest of Highway 78. Look for the sign and War Eagle Mines historical marker near milepost 34 east of Murphy, and drive carefully. The road is generally open mid-May through October and occasionally into November.

Tucked away in the Owyhee Mountains, Silver was a rollicking place from 1864 through 1875. Not only was it county seat for a vast reach of territorial southern Idaho, Silver was also home to the territory's first telegraph and the first newspaper. Telephones were in use by the 1880s, and the town was electrified in the 1890s. Silver City had its own doctors, lawyers, merchants . . . even a red-light district. During its heyday, the town had a population of 2,500 people and seventy-five businesses, all made possible by the fabulous riches on War Eagle Mountain.

All this seems unlikely—even unbelievable—today. Silver City isn't technically a ghost town, since about sixty families maintain part-time residences in the vicinity. But there are just a handful of telephones to the outside world; within town, about two dozen more run on the town's magneto crank system, reportedly the last in Idaho. There's no local mail delivery and no electricity. It's not even the county seat anymore, since that honor went to Murphy in 1935.

Silver City's charm is that it has enough amenities to make an overnight or weekend stay possible, yet it hasn't become nearly as commercialized as many other Western "ghost towns." The best way to enjoy Silver is simply to walk its dusty streets, survey the many interesting buildings, and try to imagine what life was like here more than a hundred years ago.

Two spots of particular interest are the old schoolhouse and the Idaho Hotel. Downstairs, the schoolhouse bears the various brands of the Owyhee County Cattlemen's Association, which still meets here each summer. On the back wall, former students have written their names and the years they attended the school. Upstairs, the schoolhouse has a museum, and poking through its displays is like snooping through your great-grandparents' attic. Branding irons and mining paraphernalia share space with kitchen gadgets, perfume bottles, and reminders of the Old West, such as one artifact labeled thus: "1888: J.R. Wilkins committed assault on the person of John McCabe with this pocket knife." The museum is open irregularly; call the Idaho Hotel (see below) for current operating hours.

The ◆ **Idaho Hotel** is very much a museum, too. Gorgeous antiques—an ice chest, slot machine, and pianos—vie for attention with whimsical signs and racks of guidebooks. The hotel was originally built in nearby Ruby City in 1863 and moved to Silver in 1866. After decades as a social and business center for the town, the hotel closed in 1942. Current proprietor Ed Jagels bought it in 1972 for $12,000 and reopened the historic hostelry. Although most visitors just stop in for a can of pop, a hamburger, or a few postcards, it's still possible to stay overnight in the Idaho Hotel, and Jagels has welcomed guests from as far away as Beijing, China.

The Empire Room may be the inn's finest. Used on occasion as a honeymoon suite, its furniture includes a canopy bed and a sofa that Jagels says once belonged to one of President Abraham Lincoln's bodyguards. But for all the rooms, guests must bring their own towels and bedding or sleeping bags, since the hotel has no laundry service. Woodstoves provide heat, and kerosene and twelve-volt lamps shed light. "It's like camping out with antique furniture," Jagels says. Until a few years ago, guests had to make do with chamberpots and wash basins as "facilities," but a couple of new composting toilets, sinks, and a shower are now in use.

The Idaho Hotel is open late May to late October, with rooms renting for $20 to $40 a night. Reservations are necessary, and Jagels suggests you call at least several days in advance. For more information, call Jagels at (208) 583–4104 or write The Idaho Hotel, P.O. Box 75, Murphy 83650. Jagels is also a good person to call to check on road and weather conditions before you venture to Silver. The Bureau of Land Management also has a small campground at Silver City, and its sites are free.

Back on Highway 78 watch for the signs to Oreana. Located in a scenic valley 2 miles south of the highway, Oreana has a population of 7, MAYBE 8, according to the sign at the "city limits." It's also the setting for **Our Lady, Queen of Heaven Catholic Church,** a striking stone building that started life as a general store. Mike Hyde, an area rancher, built the store from native stone in the late 1800s. When only its walls were completed, word was heard around Oreana that a war party of Indians was on its way to the town. All the local folks reportedly took refuge behind the stone walls, expecting an attack. But the Boise-based militia arrived first, and the Indians were deterred.

The store served the Oreana area well into the twentieth century, but by 1961, it had been empty and unused for some time. That year, Albert Black—on whose land it stood—gave the old building to the Catholic Diocese in Nampa. The diocese encouraged local Catholics to turn the store into a church, and Our Lady, Queen of Heaven, was the result. The picturesque church is usually locked, but you can stop by the Trading Post for the key. Inside, a sandstone slab altar sits on three steps of black slate, with tall black iron candle holders on either side. A crucifix hangs behind the altar on a sandblasted juniper tree. The sanctuary's inside walls are paneled in apa-tone wood from Japan, and the floor is of native stone, like the exterior. The small belfry atop the church houses the bell that originally hung at Our Lady of Tears in Silver City. The bell survived a 1943 flood and still rings to herald the occasional service at the church.

## SNAKE RIVER VISTAS

For a pleasant riverside picnic or some good home cooking, consider a stop at Grand View, located at the intersection of Highways 78 and 67. The town's small park has fishing access, a nature trail, and several tables overlooking the Snake River. Grand View's small city center has an old-fashioned Western boardwalk. Stop in the **Grand Owhyee Restaurant** at 210 Main Street for an Owyhee burger with beef, cheese, bacon, and ham for $4.75 or linquisa (a kind of Italian sausage) and eggs for $4.95. The Grand Owhyee also offers homemade pastries, milkshakes, and malts, along with prime rib for dinner every Friday and Saturday night. The restaurant is open from 6:00 A.M. to

10:00 P.M. during most of the year and from 7:00 A.M. to 8:00 P.M. in the winter months. The phone number is (208) 834–2200.

If all that eating makes you tired, you can bunk down in Grand View at the **Pheasant Hill Country Inn Bed and Breakfast.** Perched above C. J. Strike Reservoir, Pheasant Hill was the ranch home of Emmett Cahalan, after whom the Treasure Valley town of Emmett was named. Guests enjoy watching and photographing the local wildlife, including squirrels, ducks, white-tail deer, eagles, and pheasants, of course; fishing at the lake, which yields good catfish, trout, and bass; or just lounging in the hot tub. Three rooms with shared bath are priced at $45 to $55 for single or double occupancy. Room rates include a continental breakfast, but a full morning meal may be arranged for an additional $5.00 per person.

Mountain Home, up Highway 67, is home to an Air Force base and the bustling Gear Jammer truck stop along Interstate 84. But downtown, amid stores but tucked away on its own quiet corner, the ◆**RoseStone Inn Bed & Breakfast** is the picture of genteel elegance. Built in 1907, the early Queen Anne–style inn has five guest rooms that pay tribute to the Basque immigrants who settled in Southwestern Idaho. Rooms include telephone, cable TV, and private baths; a gift shop featuring cookbooks, candies, and Victorian novelties is also located on the premises. Rates at the RoseStone range from $35 to $65. For more information or reservations call (800) 717–ROSE, or write the RoseStone Bed & Breakfast, 495 North Third East, Mountain Home 83647.

Southeast of Mountain Home, don't miss a trip to ◆**Bruneau Dunes State Park.** Most sand dunes form at the edge of a natural basin, but these form at the center, making them unique in the Western Hemisphere. The Bruneau complex also includes the largest single structured sand dune in North America, with its peak 470 feet high. The combination of sand and a natural trap have caused sand to collect here for about 15,000 years, and the prevailing wind patterns—from the southeast 28 percent of the time and from the northwest 32 percent—ensure the dunes don't move far. The two prominent dunes cover about 600 acres.

Hiking, camping, and fishing are favorite activities at the Bruneau Dunes. Hiking to the top of a sand dune is an experience unlike any other. Once there, many hikers simply stop to savor the view before walking the crest of the dunes back to terra firma.

Others use the dunes' inside bowl for sledding, sand skiing, or snowboarding. Bass and bluegill thrive in the small lakes at the foot of the dunes, and the campground—with one of the longest seasons in Idaho—has a steady stream of visitors March through late fall. Bruneau Dunes State Park also has a good visitor center featuring displays of wildlife and natural history. Take Interstate 84 exit 95 or 112 to the dunes. A $2.00-per-vehicle park entrance fee is charged. For more information call (208) 366–7919, or write Bruneau Dunes State Park, HC 85, Box 41, Mountain Home 83647.

At what is now ◆ **Three Island Crossing State Park,** pioneers traveling west on the Oregon Trail faced the most difficult river crossing of their 2,000-mile journey. Many chose not to ford the river and continued along the south bank of the Snake River through the same country we've just traversed. But about half the emigrants decided to brave the Snake to the shorter, easier route on the river's north side. It's still possible to see the islands used in the crossing, as well as scars worn by the wagon wheels.

The crossing is re-enacted in one of Idaho's most popular annual festivals, usually held the second Saturday each August. Although the Snake isn't as mighty as it once was, fording it remains dangerous. Wagons sometimes capsize, and livestock occasionally drown. It's hard for spectators to rest easy until every man, horse, and wagon has made it across safely. Once all have, however, everyone flocks to the festival's other attractions: food, arts and crafts booths, entertainment, and the park itself. If you can't make it at crossing time, you can still enjoy Three Island's herd of bison and longhorn cattle, an informative visitor's center, and recreational activities, including camping, fishing, swimming, and picnicking. Three Island State Park is reached via exit 120 off of Interstate 84. Drive south into Glenns Ferry and follow the signs to the park. For more information call (208) 366–2394.

End your trip through Southwestern Idaho with a stop at ◆ **Carmela Winery,** right next door to Three Island Crossing State Park. Located in a building that looks like a cross between a medieval castle and a French chateau, the winery is named for Carmela Martell, who co-owns the winery with her husband, Jim. Carmela Winery's tasting room is open from 11:00 A.M. to 5:00 P.M. daily, with tours available by request. The winery produces Riesling, Semillion, Chardonnay, Muscat Canelli, Lemberger, Cabernet Sauvignon, and Amanda's Blush, named after Carmela's mother. The wines are also featured in the on-site Royal Vineyard Restaurant, with its panoramic view of the Snake River. The restaurant is open from 7:00 A.M. to 10:00 P.M. for breakfast, lunch, and dinner. After your meal, browse the adjacent gift shop's good selection of artwork, books, and Idaho products.

Carmela may very well be the only winery with a golf course right on the premises, too. A nine-hole course was added a few years ago. Fees are $8.00 for nine holes and $14.00 for eighteen holes, with gas and pull carts available. If Three Island's campground is full, try the RV park adjacent to Carmela. For more information on the winery, call (208) 366–2313.

# SOUTH CENTRAL IDAHO

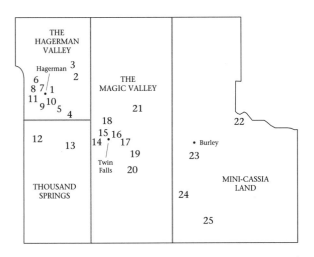

1. Malad Gorge State Park
2. Gooding Hotel
3. Gooding City of Rocks
4. Niagara Springs
5. Thousand Springs Preserve
6. Teater's Knoll
7. Cary House Bed & Breakfast
8. Snake River Pottery
9. River Bank Restaurant
10. Rose Creek Winery
11. Hagerman Fossil Beds National Monument
12. Balanced Rock
13. Clover Lutheran Church
14. Metropolis Bakery Cafe
15. Herrett Museum
16. Snake River Canyon
17. Evel Knievel Launch Site
18. Idaho Farm and Ranch Museum
19. Shoshone Falls
20. Rock Creek Stage Station
21. Hunt Camp
22. Lake Walcott Park
23. Cassia County Historical Museum
24. Oakley
25. City of Rocks National Reserve

# SOUTH CENTRAL IDAHO
## THE HAGERMAN VALLEY

To the casual traveler along Interstate 84, South Central Idaho seems an arid, apparently barren expanse on the way to somewhere else. To many visitors, the best show seems to be in the sky, where clouds march over wide vistas hemmed by distant mountain peaks.

This big landscape hides its treasures well, but they're really not hard to find. In many cases the region's best-kept secrets are just a few miles off the interstate, and in the case of Malad Gorge, the highway literally passes right overhead.

At Malad Gorge, the Big Wood River becomes the Malad River, tumbling into a canyon 250 feet deep and just 140 feet wide. This area, called the Devil's Washbowl, is the centerpiece of ◆ **Malad Gorge State Park,** a wonderfully handy spot for a break from the interstate. To get there, take exit 147 at Tuttle.

"Malad" is French for "sick," and Malad Gorge got its name when nineteenth-century fur trappers became ill after eating beaver caught nearby. The Malad River itself is thought to be one of the world's shortest, running just two and a half miles before being swallowed up by the mighty Snake River downstream. A short trail from the main parking area leads to a footbridge over the plunge. Wagon-wheel ruts from the Kelton Road, an old freight route from Utah to Idaho, may be seen nearby, as may traces of the old stage stop. Park staff discovered these several years ago while cleaning up a local garbage dump. Malad Gorge has facilities for hiking and picnicking, but no camping is permitted. The park's roads are excellent for walking, jogging, or bicycling; indeed, this is the site of a popular annual run held the Saturday before each St. Patrick's Day. Most days, however, you'll likely have the place to yourself. For more information on Malad Gorge, call (208) 837–4505.

From Malad Gorge, it's a short drive to Gooding—the county seat and home of the only American Youth Hostel–recognized facility in southern Idaho, the ◆ **Gooding Hotel** at 112 Main. As such, the hotel attracts many international travelers en route to Sun Valley or Yellowstone National Park. Gooding is an old railroad town, and the hotel was built right by the tracks not long after the town's founding about 1883. Then as now, its location was ideal, within walking distance of Gooding's restaurants, bars, and shops. Modern vagabonds can choose from the spartan hostel accommodations, priced at $9.00 to $12.00 per person per night or the slightly more luxurious (and almost as cheap) hotel rooms of this old railroad way station. Rooms 7 and 14 are among the nicest; the cost is $38, which includes a full breakfast served in a room brimming with Gooding memorabilia. For more information or reservations, call (208) 934–4374. If you're in Gooding in midsummer, don't miss the annual Basque Picnic, usually served the third Sunday of July at West Park. The event includes a barbecue of lamb chops, chorizos (a highly seasoned pork sausage), beans, rice, and more, plus dancing, music, and games.

Northwest of town off of State Highway 46, the ◆ **Gooding City of Rocks** offers a panorama of highly eroded canyon lands, Native American petroglyphs, and spring wildflowers. The area—which shouldn't be confused with the City of Rocks National Reserve, its more famous cousin south of Burley (see page 82)—is located west off of Highway 46. It's particularly appealing to kids, who will have a ball exploring the fantastic rock formations. Keep an eye out for the elk herds who live on the high desert lands nearby. Highway 46 continues north to a sweeping vista of the Camas Prairie, its blue flowers usually in bloom shortly before Memorial Day.

South of Gooding the town of Wendell provides access to both sides of the Snake River Canyon and to the Hagerman Valley, where recreation and relaxation are a way of life. But since Snake River crossings are few and far between here, we'll first take a look at some north- and east-rim attractions that are best accessed from Interstate 84.

A new Idaho state park that is actually a satellite of Malad Gorge, Niagara Springs State Park has also been designated a National Natural Landmark. One of the last and largest remaining springs in an area that still bears the "Thousand Springs" name it received from Oregon-bound pioneers, ◆ **Niagara Springs** churns from the Snake River Canyon wall at 250 cubic feet per second.

Niagara Springs is a splendid spot for picnics and wildlife watching, especially waterfowl. Kids and senior citizens can fish for free at the nearby **Crystal Springs Fish Hatchery,** a commercial operation. To reach the Niagara Springs/Crystal Springs area, take Interstate 84 exit 157 from Wendell and drive south on the Rex Leland Highway to the canyon rim. The steep, narrow road here drops 350 feet and is not suitable for large RVs or trailers.

Not far west, The Nature Conservancy has established its ◆ **Thousand Springs Preserve** on Ritter Island in the Snake River. The seventy-acre island was once owned by Utah-based businesswoman Minnie Miller, who established what became one of the nation's top guernsey cattle herds right on this site. Tours of the grounds are offered most Saturdays during the summer and an arts festival takes place each fall. Call (208) 536–6797 for a schedule and detailed directions to the preserve.

Hagerman itself is accessible via Highway 30 south from Bliss or north from Buhl and via the Vader Grade west from Wendell. With its year-round mild climate and abundant recreation, the Hagerman Valley offers many pleasures, and it's easy to enjoy several diversions on any given day. Fishing is a major lure, with some of the state's most productive waters—the Snake River, Billingsley Creek, Oster Lakes, and the Anderson Ponds—located nearby. Floating is another popular pastime, and rafters can often take to the Snake as early as April 1 (and as late as Halloween), with the area just below the Lower Salmon Falls Power Plant the most popular spot to put in. Many people navigate this stretch on their own, but at least two companies—**High Adventure River Tours** at (208) 733–0123 and **Hagerman Valley Outfitters** at (208) 837–6100—offer guided white-water floats. **Thousand Springs Tours** specializes in scenic floats on calmer waters in the area. Call (208) 837–9006 for information.

A float trip below Lower Salmon Falls is the best way to sneak a peak at ◆ **Teater's Knoll,** the only Idaho structure designed by Frank Lloyd Wright. The home and studio, which are perched high above the Snake, were built for Western artist Archie Teater and his wife, Patricia, who lived there part-time from the late 1950s through the 1970s. The home, later purchased and restored by modern-day Idaho architect Henry Whiting, is on the National Register of Historic Places. It is presently inaccessible to the public.

Hagerman has several selections for overnight lodging. One, the ◆ **Cary House Bed & Breakfast,** houses guests from all over the West amid Victorian-era antiques. All rooms come with a full gourmet breakfast that might include such fare as souffléed apple pancakes, quiche, or Grand Marnier French toast. "We try to serve things they might not get at home," says Linda Heinemann, who runs the inn with her husband, Darrell. "We spoil 'em real bad." Rooms at the Cary House range from $55 to $75; call (208) 837–4848 for reservations. The inn is located one-half mile north of Hagerman on U.S. Highway 30.

The Hagerman Valley continues to attract more than its share of creative people, bolstering the area's growing reputation as a center for the arts. One worthwhile stop is ❖**Snake River Pottery,** just down the Old Bliss Grade west of the Malad River bridge. The pottery was started in 1947 by Drich and Di Bowler, self-taught artists who also traveled the state in a school bus performing classical dramas as the Antique Festival Theater. Di passed away in 1986, but her husband has kept the pottery in business with the help of younger artisans. **Advance-to-Go Stained Glass** on State Street, Hagerman's main drag, is also worth a peek; the shop, open Tuesday through Saturday, features clothing, furniture, antiques, and jewelry as well as stained-glass arts.

If you're hungry, Hagerman's best choice is the ❖**River Bank Restaurant,** an unpretentious spot where owners Bud, Barbara, and Jeff Deakins serve up Idaho, Ozark, and Cajun-style cooking that can't be beat. The restaurant is housed in a former bank, and the family's recipes are "guarded" in a vault that's still in place. Visitors waiting for dinner can have fun checking out the many photographs of sturgeon taken from the Snake River. The largest of these monster fish grow to be 8 feet, weigh 150 pounds or more, and live almost as long as humans.

The River Bank's specialties are fresh trout and catfish accompanied by hush puppies and fried green tomatoes. Occasional specials, prepared when the right ingredients are available, have included sturgeon, Cajun barbecued shrimp, and jambalaya. Save room for dessert; the Deakinses's pies, cakes, and cobblers are positively legendary in these parts. Entrées range from $5.95 to $15.95, with sandwiches and "tadpole" meals for kids and seniors priced less. For hours and information call (208) 837–6462 or (800) 303–4347. The River Bank is located at 191 North State.

❖**Rose Creek Winery** is another popular place to duck into. Although just founded in the mid-1980s, Rose Creek is one of Idaho's oldest wineries and has won numerous awards for its varieties, some of which are sold only at the winery. The tasting room is located in the basement of a century-old stone building at 111 West Hagerman Avenue and is open daily from 11:30 A.M. to 5:30 P.M. except Thanksgiving, Christmas, and Easter. Mid-fall, when the grape harvest is under way, is the best time to visit. Call (208) 837–4413 for harvest updates or more information.

As if all this wasn't enough to entice visitors to Hagerman, the town is host to one of the nation's newest National Parks units. The ◆ **Hagerman Fossil Beds National Monument** marks the spot where an area farmer discovered fossils that turned out to be those of the zebralike Hagerman Horse, now the official Idaho state fossil. In the 1930s, the Smithsonian Institution sent several expeditions to collect specimens of the horse. Archaeologists unearthed 130 skulls and 15 skeletons of an early, zebralike horse that dated back to the Pliocene Age about 3.4 million years ago. Other fossils in the area preserved early forms of camel, peccary, beaver, turtle, and freshwater fish.

For the first few years after its establishment in 1988, Hagerman Fossil Beds National Monument didn't offer much in the way of interpretation. That's slowly changing; the site now has a visitor center located in town at 221 North State, several wayside exhibits, and a regular summer schedule of tours on different topics ranging from archaeology to astronomy to the Oregon Trail, which passed through the area. For more information or a schedule, call (208) 837–4793.

## THOUSAND SPRINGS

South of Hagerman, U.S. Highway 30 enters Twin Falls County. The highway here is known as the **Thousand Springs Scenic Route,** taking its name from the white cascades that gush from the black basalt of the Snake River Canyon. At one time, there probably were truly a thousand springs, give or take a few. Today, there are far fewer, but the sight remains impressive.

Where do the springs originate? Many have traveled hundreds of miles underground from eastern Idaho, where the Big Lost River and several other streams abruptly sink underground. From there, the water moves ever so slowly, possibly just 10 feet a day, through the Snake River Aquifer before bursting forth from the canyon walls. Hot springs are also abundant in the area, and several resorts line Highway 30 between Hagerman and Buhl.

Most offer swimming, camping, and picnic facilities; at least two (**Banbury Hot Springs** and **Miracle Hot Springs**) boast private VIP baths. **Sligar's 1000 Springs Resort** has swimming year-round.

South Central Idaho produces a whopping 90 percent of the world's commercially raised trout, and **Clear Springs Foods**—by far the largest of the trout processors—offers a glimpse at the fish business at its visitor center north of Buhl on the Snake River. In Buhl itself, the little coffeehouse/bookstore **Cosmic Jolt** at 120 South Broadway provides a taste of the metaphysical in this unlikely farm-town setting. **Smith's Dairy,** another local institution at 205 South Broadway, scoops up Al & Reed's, the ice cream made from potatoes in Idaho Falls. Enjoy a cone in the gazebo just outside.

A short drive southwest of Buhl leads to ◆**Balanced Rock,** a curious geological formation that seems poised like a giant mushroom (or maybe a question mark?) against the blue Idaho sky. The landmark is just a few miles west of Castleford, and a nearby small county park along Salmon Falls Creek provides the perfect spot for a picnic. To get there, follow the signs out of Buhl for 16 miles.

Clover, a small farming community due east of Castleford, is the setting for one of Idaho's most beautiful country churches. ◆**Clover Lutheran Church** has long served the families of the area, and the parishioners have given back to the church in equal measure, most notably through the stained-glass windows that grace the north and south sides of the sanctuary. These windows, done in traditional leaded stained-glass style, were made entirely by members of the congregation. The windows on the south side depict the local farming community, including sprigs of clover; those on the north are rich in Christian symbolism. The church also has its original ceiling of embossed tin.

Sunday mornings would be the best time to see Clover Lutheran, hear its pipe organ, and visit with the congregation. But the church is worth a stop at any time. If no one's in the office on the building's northwest side, check at the parsonage, located at the ranch house just to the north. The church cemetery is also notable for its headstones, some of which are in the native German of the people who settled Clover. The oldest graves are in the cemetery's southwest corner.

**Balanced Rock**

Farm fanciers may wish to linger a bit longer in the Buhl-Clover area to see several beautiful barns. (Find the 1700 East Road, 1 mile west of Clover or 2 miles east of Buhl. Head north from Clover or south from Highway 30.) Henry Schick was the man responsible for many of Twin Falls County's early barns, including at least three seen here: the Maxwell barn, built in 1910, on the east side of the road; Schick's own barn, on the west side down the road a piece; and the concrete Kunze barn just south of Schick's spread.

Filer is home to the **Twin Falls County Fair,** which the *Los Angeles Times* recently named one of the top ten county fairs in the United States. The fair, which runs the six days up to and including Labor Day, is big enough to draw top-name country singers and rodeo cowboys, yet small enough to retain a real down-home feel. The "Filer Fair," as it's known locally, also provides a ready excuse to forget your diet for a while: Check out the Job's Daughter's elephant-ear scones (deep-fried dough topped with cinnamon sugar), the one-of-a-kind troutburgers served up by the Buhl Catholic Church, or the tater pigs—a link sausage stuffed inside an Idaho baked potato—offered by the Magichords, a local barbershop singing group.

Just east of Filer, U.S. Highway 93 swings south from Highway 30 for the Nevada border some 40 miles away. First, however, the traveler comes to Hollister and Rogerson. The **Idaho Heritage Museum,** located between the two towns, is known for its collection of mounted big-game animals and Native American artifacts, while nearby **Nat-Soo-Pah Hot Springs** is a popular soaking spot on hot summer days.

Farther south, just over the Nevada line, **Jackpot** serves as the gambling hub for Idaho (and, judging from license plates in the casino parking lots, for revelers from as far away as Montana, Manitoba, and Saskatchewan, too). The town's biggest draw is **Cactus Pete's,** a full-fledged resort with comfortable rooms, abundant dining options (including the Plateau Room, possibly the classiest restaurant in a 100-mile radius), and semi-big-name entertainment. But some folks prefer the down-home, distinctly non-Vegas atmosphere of the town's smaller casinos, especially **Barton's Club 93.**

Highway 93 is also the best jumping-off spot for the Jarbidge country, one of the West's most wild and remote areas. Although

**75**

on the border like Jackpot, Jarbidge's main attraction isn't gambling but natural splendor: the **Jarbidge Mountains** boast eight peaks higher than 10,000 feet, the highest concentration in Nevada; and campers, hikers, and horseback riders will swear they've found paradise. The town itself has about three dozen homes, a couple of cafes, and the **Tshawawbitts Lodge,** a bed and breakfast originally built by New York City publishing magnate Roscoe Fawcett in the 1970s. Rooms run about $65 a night for two people. To get to Jarbidge, take the road west from Rogerson. All but the last 17 miles are paved. Call (702) 488–2338 for more information or reservations (a must).

## THE MAGIC VALLEY

Back on Route 30, the traveler reaches Twin Falls, the largest city in South Central Idaho. The city's main commercial strip, Blue Lakes Boulevard, is packed with chain restaurants and motels, but the still-thriving downtown area offers more relaxed, unique alternatives (at least for dining and shopping; Blue Lakes and Addison Avenue provide better selections for lodging).

Downtown Twin Falls is at its liveliest near the corner of Main Avenue and Shoshone. **Dunken's Draught House,** a friendly, well-lit tavern at the intersection, is the local version of *Cheers,* but with a decidedly Idaho flavor. Proprietor Tim Jones presides over an excellent selection of beers and ales from the Northwest and beyond, and the walls—a veritable capsule history of Twin Falls—are a sight to see.

Two of Twin Falls' best eateries are located just down the street. **The Uptown Bistro** at 117 Main Avenue East features sidewalk dining in season and a creative menu leaning toward Cajun and Creole specialties, all quite reasonably priced. ◆**Metropolis Bakery Cafe** at 125 Main Avenue East is a good spot to sip espresso, read a magazine, view changing art displays, and sample the award-winning pastries of Susan Ettesvold, who co-owns the cafe with her husband, Eric. The Metropolis is open from 8:00 A.M. to 6:00 P.M. Monday through Thursday and Saturday, and from 8:00 A.M. to 11:00 P.M. Friday. Its phone number is (208) 734–4457. For shopping try **The Leatherman,** just across the street at 138 Main Avenue South. This funky little store lures patrons from as far away as Sun Valley and Boise for its unusual footwear, clothing, jewelry, books, and more.

A bit more out of the way is the **Buffalo Cafe,** where locals stampede for a breakfast voted the best in town. Many patrons favor a heaping helping of the house specialty, Buffalo Chips, a mixture of sliced spuds, eggs, bacon, green chiles, tomatoes, and onions, all smothered in cheese and sour cream. You'll find the Buffalo at 218 Fourth Avenue West in the city's long-neglected Old Town district, which is now undergoing a revival. Another spot worth checking out while you're in the neighborhood is **My Grandfather's Attic,** housed in what was once a creamery at 702 Third Street West. The shop specializes in country-style furniture and American-made goods including quilts, rugs, folk art prints, and other elegantly rustic home accessories.

Twin Falls is the home of the **College of Southern Idaho,** a rapidly growing junior college known for its championship basketball team and for the ◆ **Herrett Museum.** This fine facility houses a remarkable collection of Indian artifacts from North and Central America. The Herrett is also adding a planetarium due to open in late 1995; it will be one of only about two dozen in the world using the state-of-the-art Digistar projection system. With it, the Herrett will be able to beam everything from star shows to computer-generated DNA helixes, dinosaur skeletons, and art masterworks on the planetarium dome. The Herrett's hours are 9:30 A.M. to 8:00 P.M. Tuesday, 9:30 A.M. to 4:30 P.M. Wednesday through Friday, and 1:00 to 4:30 P.M. Saturday. For more information or a planetarium update, call (208) 733-9554.

Few towns can match Twin Falls for an impressive "front door," in this case, the majestic ◆ **Snake River Canyon.** The canyon was created by the Bonneville Flood, which came roaring from prehistoric Lake Bonneville through southeastern Idaho's Red Rock Pass tens of thousands of years ago. At its peak, the flood spewed 15 million cubic feet of water per second, or three times the flow of the Amazon River, carving the massive canyon that now serves as Twin Falls's welcome mat. The gorge is spanned by the Perrine Bridge, a 1,500-foot-long engineering marvel standing 486 feet above the river. When the first Perrine bridge was completed in 1927, it was the highest cantilever bridge for its length in the world. The present span was completed in 1976, and visitors can view the canyon from overlooks on either rim or from a walkway on the bridge itself.

The **Buzz Langdon Visitor Center** on the south rim is staffed by helpful senior citizen volunteers who can point out such attractions as the ◆ **Evel Knievel Launch Site,** from which the daredevil attempted his famous September 1974 rocket-cycle leap across the canyon. (He failed, only to parachute to the river below.) Also visible from the rim or the bridge are two of America's prettiest golf courses: **Canyon Springs Golf Course** (open to the public) and **Blue Lakes Country Club** (which is private). The visitor center staff would be pleased to tell you why this part of Idaho is known as the Magic Valley. Southern Idaho is one of the most productive farming areas in the United States, but it would be little more than a desert were it not for the Snake River. Several massive irrigation projects fostered early in the twentieth century turned the desert into rich agricultural land, just like "magic." Pick up a self-guiding agricultural tour brochure to see such area crops as beans, barley, sugar beets, and those famous Idaho potatoes.

The ◆ **Idaho Farm and Ranch Museum,** just up U.S. Highway 93 from Twin Falls at the Interstate 84 interchange, is another good place to explore the history of irrigated farming. The museum is presently a work in progress, but plans call for the eventual additions of a pioneer town Main Street, a petting zoo for children, and a nature trail. A wide variety of old-time agricultural implements and a 1909 settler's "prove-up" shack are already on display.

A few miles east of Twin Falls, ◆ **Shoshone Falls** ranks among Idaho's most impressive sights. Sometimes called the Niagara of the West, this cataract is actually 212 feet tall, or 45 feet higher than Niagara Falls. It is best viewed in springtime before much of the Snake River's runoff is diverted for the aforementioned agricultural irrigation. But Shoshone Falls/Dierkes Lake park is well worth a visit any time of year. Swimming, fishing, rock climbing, picnicking, and boating are among the available activities, and an easy hike back to Dierkes's "hidden lakes" is most pleasant.

This is Oregon Trail country, and one trading post used by the emigrants—the ◆ **Rock Creek Stage Station**—can still be seen 5 miles south of Hansen. (Follow the signs off of Highway 30 east of Twin Falls.) Built in 1865 by James Bascom, the log store at the site is the oldest building in South Central Idaho.

**Rock Creek Stage Station**

Interpretive signs tell how the site (also called Stricker Ranch, after a later owner) served the pioneers at the intersection of the Oregon Trail, Ben Holladay's Overland Stage route, and the Kelton Road from Utah. Shaded picnic facilities are available. Poke around on your own, or arrange a tour by calling (208) 733–8753.

The road south from Hansen continues along Rock Creek into the Twin Falls district of the Sawtooth National Forest, known locally as the **South Hills.** Long considered a private playground by Twin Falls–area residents, the South Hills offer good trails for hiking, horses, cross-country skiing, all-terrain vehicles, and snowmobiles. Facilities include several campgrounds and picnic areas, along with the small, family-run **Magic Mountain Ski Area.** Call the Forest Service office at (208) 737–3200 for more information; a regularly updated recorded recreation report for the entire Sawtooth National Forest can be heard by calling (208) 737–3250.

During World War II, more than 110,000 American citizens of Japanese descent were rounded up from the West Coast and incarcerated farther inland. Many from the Seattle area were transported to the Minidoka War Relocation Center, or ◈ **Hunt Camp,** as it came to be known. At one time, nearly 10,000 people lived at Hunt, making it Idaho's eighth-largest city. Conditions in the camp were less than ideal. People lived in cramped tar-paper shacks. Guards were posted and prisoners told they would be shot if they moved too close to the barbed-wire fences. Despite the hardship and indignities, about one in ten camp residents wound up serving in the U.S. Armed Forces during World War II.

Little remains of the camp, but visitors can see the waiting room and guard station, both made of lava. A plaque nearby pays tribute to residents who died in the war, and another shows the layout of the camp. Of particular note are the half-dozen or so ball diamonds—the prisoners found some solace and entertainment in pick-up baseball games—and the fields where evacuees grew various crops for the war effort. The camp site is located a little more than 2 miles north of State Highway 25, 7 miles west of Eden. A pair of Idaho highway historical signs—one on Hunt, the other on Prehistoric Man—marks the turn. The Prehistoric Man sign refers to nearby Wilson Butte Cave, a major archaeological site. Artifacts from this cave have been carbon dated at 14,500 years old, making them among the oldest findings in the New World. There are no interpretive displays at the cave, but it can be found by driving 2 miles north of the Hunt Camp, then 3.7 miles west. Here the road turns to dirt and, in 2 more miles, crosses a canal. A sign another half-mile or so down the road points the way to the cave, still 2 miles away.

Lava is the dominant feature of the landscape north of the Snake River Canyon. North and east of Shoshone, the Lincoln County seat, the roadways are rimmed with rugged **lava flows** that rolled over the land between 2,000 and 15,000 years ago. Some are lava tubes, created when a shell formed around a still-flowing river of lava. When the lava moved on, the shell remained. The Shoshone office of the Bureau of Land Management can provide information on exploring these lava tubes; call

(208) 886–2206. **Idaho's Mammoth Cave** and **Shoshone Indian Ice Caves** are commercially run operations offering a glimpse at the lava's handiwork; both are located north of Shoshone on Highway 75.

The **Governors Mansion Bed & Breakfast** at Highway 75 and South Greenwood Street in Shoshone earned its name because owners Edie Collins and Marge Clark originally believed the stately home was built by Frank Gooding, an early Idaho governor. Gooding's brother, Thomas, was actually the man responsible, but the name stuck. The inn has a variety of accommodations ranging from the Pink Room, suitable for a special occasion, to a basement bunkhouse, which is able to sleep six people at $20 per bed. Call (208) 886–2858 for more information or reservations.

## MINI-CASSIA LAND

Word is getting out about ◆ **Lake Walcott Park**, a high-desert oasis situated along the portion of the Snake River impounded by Minidoka Dam. The park is located within the **Minidoka National Wildlife Refuge,** where migratory waterfowl including ducks, geese, and tundra swans stop on their fall and spring journeys. Recent improvements at the site have helped Lake Walcott better cater to campers, horseback riders, picnickers, and growing ranks of windsurfers. The park is located 10 miles northeast of Rupert on State Highway 24.

**Minidoka Dam** itself is also worth a look. Built starting in 1904, the dam became the first federal hydroelectric power project in the Northwest. Minidoka and later dams made possible the irrigation and settlement of southern Idaho's fertile but dry soil. A new power house is now under construction, and tours at the site will resume when it is completed, probably in 1997.

A loop drive through Cassia County takes the traveler back in time to one of the West's best-preserved towns, mountain scenery, and a world-class rock-climbing area. To begin head south on State Highway 27 from Burley, the county seat. Burley is best known for the **Idaho Regatta,** a major powerboating event held annually the last weekend of June. Lesser known and a lot more quiet, but just as fascinating, is the ◆ **Cassia County His-**

**torical Museum** at East Main Street and Highland Avenue, where a large map documents the area's many pioneer trails. Other exhibits tell of Idaho's farming, ranching, mining, and logging history. The museum is open 10:00 A.M. to 5:00 P.M. Tuesday through Saturday, April through mid-November. Call (208) 678–7172 for more information.

The small town of ◆ **Oakley** was settled around 1878 by Mormon pioneers and is famous for its impressive collection of fine historic buildings. In fact, all of Oakley has been designated a National Historic District, with particularly notable landmarks including the Marcus Funk residence, the Oakley Co-op, and Howells Castle. Benjamin Howells, an early settler and judge, also built Howells Opera House, where the Oakley Valley Arts Council continues to present musical performances to this day. Visit Oakley's city park for a look at a jail cell that once housed the notorious Diamondfield Jack (more on him in a moment).

The peaks rising to Oakley's east are the Albion Mountains, the highest in South Central Idaho. Inquire locally or call the Sawtooth National Forest's Burley Ranger District at (208) 678–0430 for directions into the high country. Day hikers and backpackers alike will enjoy a trek to **Independence Lakes,** four tiny blue gems tucked against 10,339-foot Cache Peak. **Lake Cleveland,** another locally popular outdoor playground atop adjacent Mount Harrison, may be accessed by motor vehicle. Camping, picnicking, and fishing are favorite pastimes here. **Pomerelle,** a family-friendly ski area featuring about two dozen runs and the region's only nighttime skiing, is also located on Mount Harrison. Call (208) 638–5555 for the ski report or (208) 638–5599 for the resort office.

Southeast of Oakley, Emery Canyon Road provides access to the ◆ **City of Rocks National Reserve.** This 14,300-acre area was named by California Trail pioneers passing through in the mid-nineteenth century, some of whom marked their names in axle grease on the ancient granite formations. "During the afternoon, we passed through a stone village composed of huge, isolated rocks of various and singular shapes, some resembling cottages, others steeples and domes," wrote Margaret Frink, who visited in 1850. "It is called City of Rocks, but I think the name Pyramid City more suitable. It is a sublime, strange, and wonderful scene—one of nature's most interesting works."

The City of Rocks's hoodoos, arches, caves, and monoliths are the result of erosion, not earthquakes or volcanic activity as some visitors suppose. Most of the rock is part of the Almo Pluton formation, about 25 million years old, while some is part of the 2.5-billion-year-old Green Creek Complex, among the oldest rock in the continental United States. Both kinds can easily be seen at the Twin Sisters formation. The darker "twin" is the older rock, the lighter is from the younger formation.

Today's City of Rocks is in a state of steady but certain development, much of it prompted by the legions of rock climbers who come here to scale the City's challenging spires, some sixty to seventy stories high. In addition to climbers and history buffs, the City beckons stargazers (who value the pitch-black sky), campers, mountain bikers, cross-country skiers, and sightseers. For more information call (208) 824–5519 or stop by the reserve office in nearby Almo, the City's eastern gateway.

From Almo, the Cassia County loop and State Highway 77 resume at the crossroads town of Connor. Head north 11 miles to Albion, site of the **Diamondfield Jack Davis** trial. It was here Davis was found guilty in 1897 of murdering two sheepmen in a range war skirmish. Other men later confessed to the killings, but Davis was sentenced to hang, narrowly escaping the gallows not once but twice before his eventual pardon. Davis moved to Nevada and became a successful miner, only to squander his wealth and die in 1949 after being hit by a Las Vegas taxicab.

Albion is also notable as the former home of the **Albion State Normal School,** one of Idaho's leading teacher-training colleges. The school's beautiful campus later housed a Christian college; today, local residents are restoring the grounds. An arts and crafts festival and campus reunion are held at the site the first weekend each August. From Albion, it's 12 miles north to Interstate 84.

# SOUTHEASTERN IDAHO

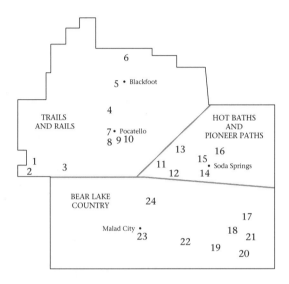

6

5 • Blackfoot

4

TRAILS
AND RAILS

7 • Pocatello
8 9 10

HOT BATHS
AND
PIONEER PATHS

13

15    16

11         • Soda Springs
12    14

1
2    3

BEAR LAKE
COUNTRY                24

17

Malad City •         18
23                21
22         19
20

1. Massacre Rocks State Park
2. Register Rock
3. Bowen Canyon Bald Eagle
   Sanctuary
4. Fort Hall Indian Reservation
5. Idaho's World Potato
   Exposition
6. Hell's Half Acre Lava Field
7. Continental Bistro
8. Standrod House
9. Fort Hall Replica
10. Bannock County Historical
    Museum
11. Olympic Swimming Complex

12. Lava Hot Pools
13. Chesterfield
14. Oregon Trail Golf Course
15. Geyser Park
16. Formation Springs
17. Rails and Trails Museum
18. Paris Stake Tabernacle
19. Minnetonka Cave
20. Bear Lake
21. Bear Lake National Wildlife
    Refuge
22. Deer Cliff Inn
23. Iron Door Playhouse
24. Downata Hot Springs Resort

# SOUTHEASTERN IDAHO
## TRAILS AND RAILS

Southeastern Idaho serves as a microcosm of the history of American westward expansion. It was here that pioneers had to decide whether to jump off onto the California Trail for the gold country. It was here many others came north from Utah, following their Mormon leaders' orders to farm the land and settle new towns. And it was here many pressed on toward Oregon, pausing briefly for supplies and rest before crossing the rugged Snake River Plain.

Power County has two sites as interesting to modern explorers as they were to the travelers of yore. Most pioneer wagon trains traversed southern Idaho without trouble from the Indians. But as traffic along the trail increased, the native peoples grew ever more resentful of the whites invading their land. This may have been the impetus for an August 1862 incident that led to the deaths of ten westward-bound emigrants and an unknown number of Shoshones in two days of fighting amid the lava outcroppings along the Snake River. During the emigrant era, the area became known as the Gate of Death or Devil's Gate because of a narrow, rocky passage through which the wagons rolled (now gone as a result of blasting for the construction of Interstate 86). But stories of the 1862 battles eventually led the locals to dub the area Massacre Rocks.

◆ **Massacre Rocks State Park,** situated on a narrow strip of land between Interstate 86 and the Snake River, has made the most of its location. Hikers can trace history or see more than 200 species of birds and 300 varieties of desert plants along nearly 7 miles of trails. The park also has notable geologic features, many the result of extensive volcanic activity, others created by the massive Bonneville Flood, the second-largest flood in world geologic history. But things are quieter today. In addition to hiking, fishing, boating, and searching out the local flora and fauna, visitors can spend a peaceful respite in the park's campground, where nightly campfire programs are held each summer. Those making a brief stop in the area can combine a hike with a stop in the visitors center. Exhibits include the diary of Jane A. Gould, who traveled from Iowa to California in 1862 along the Oregon Trail and was in the area at the time of the skirmish with the Shoshones. For more information on Massacre Rocks, call (208) 548–2672.

◆ **Register Rock,** located a few miles west of Massacre Rocks, was a favorite campground along the Oregon Trail, and many visiting emigrants signed their names on a large basalt boulder that is now the centerpiece of a small park. Some signatures date back as early as 1849, and many are still legible. On a smaller rock nearby, J. J. Hansen, a seven-year-old emigrant boy, carved an Indian's head in 1866. Nearly five decades later, after he had become a professional sculptor, Hansen returned and dated the rock again.

Register Rock's shady picnic area offers welcome relief from the searing Idaho summer. But if your visit comes in winter, consider a guided cross-country ski trek through the ◆ **Bowen Canyon Bald Eagle Sanctuary.** The canyon serves as a night roosting area for bald eagles who winter each year along the Snake River. Kent Rudeen, whose family has ranched the surrounding land for several generations, has developed about 7 miles of groomed ski trails in and around the sanctuary. The main trail is about 2 miles long and easily traveled by even beginning skiers. Once in the sanctuary, visitors can see as many as forty-five eagles soar amid the old-growth fir trees, play tag, and communicate with each other in a lively chatter. Many skiers head into the canyon about 4:00 P.M. to see the eagles' arrival, then return by the light of a headlamp, flashlight, or full moon. But visitors have the option of staying overnight in the small, heated Skiers' Roost cabin, which sleeps four to six people and comes complete with cooking facilities. For rates or reservations call (208) 226–5591 or write to Rudeen Ranch, 612 Calder, American Falls 83211.

For an interesting detour off the interstate between American Falls and Blackfoot, consider taking **State Highway 39.** This 55-mile route (as opposed to 47 miles via the interstate) offers a pleasant two-lane alternative through several small towns and a lot of pretty potato country on the north side of American Falls Reservoir. Watch for the signs showing access to fishing on the manmade lake.

South and east of the reservoir, many Native Americans from the Shoshone and Bannock tribes live on the ◆ **Fort Hall Indian Reservation,** which stretches across much of Power,

Bannock, and Bingham counties. Fort Hall is the most populous of Idaho's four reservations, with about 3,000 people living within its boundaries. A tribal museum explains that history and offers tours of the reservation by request. For more information or to book a tour, call (208) 237–9791.

The **Shoshone-Bannock Indian Festival** and **All-Indian Rodeos** are held the second week of each August, and the tribes also operate a number of small businesses, including a truck stop and trading post complex at exit 80 off of Interstate 15. Browse at the **Clothes Horse Trading Post,** which features a good selection of Indian beadwork, craft items, and cassette tapes by Native American musicians. Or eat at the **Oregon Trail Restaurant,** where the specialties include buffalo burgers, buffalo steaks, eggs and buffalo sausage, buffalo stew, and fry bread. The restaurant is open daily from 6:00 A.M. to midnight. Its phone number is (208) 237–0472.

Blackfoot, located just north of the reservation, narrowly lost an 1880 bid to replace Boise as capital of the Idaho Territory. Instead, Blackfoot has become the Potato Capital of Idaho and probably the world. Potatoes have long been synonymous with Idaho, and Blackfoot is the seat and largest town in Bingham County, the state's top spud-producing region. Small wonder, then, that Blackfoot's top attraction is ◆ **Idaho's World Potato Exposition,** dedicated to "fun and educational exhibits about the world's most popular vegetable." The world's largest potato chip—25 inches by 14 inches—is on display, as is a photo of Marilyn Monroe modeling an Idaho potato sack. The center also offers "Free Taters for Out-of-Staters," one free baked Idaho potato to eat after touring the exhibits. A snack bar also offers such treats as potato ice cream (made by Reed's Dairy; see Idaho Falls), potato cookies, and potato fudge. Picnic grounds are available.

The Potato Expo is located in downtown Blackfoot at 130 Northwest Main Street, in the old train depot. (Watch for the Burma Shave-style roadside signs extolling the Expo and the potato's many virtues as you approach the Blackfoot exits on Interstate 15!) Hours are 10:00 A.M. to 7:00 P.M. Monday through Saturday, May through October, or by appointment. A $2.00-per-person donation is suggested ($1.00 for AAA members). For more information call (208) 785–2517.

North of Blackfoot, travelers will notice the vast lava beds to the west. ◈ **Hell's Half Acre Lava Field,** located midway between Blackfoot and Idaho Falls, is a 180-square-mile flow that has been designated a National Natural Landmark. This is a relatively young lava field, with the last eruptions probably taking place about 2,000 years ago (although the flows near the interstate are probably twice that old). Hikers have two options here: a short educational loop trail (marked by blue-topped poles) that takes about a half-hour to traverse, or a 4½-mile route that leads to the vent, or source, of the lava flow. The way to the vent is marked by red-topped poles, and the hike takes a full day. Be sure to wear boots with sturdy soles and carry plenty of water.

Pocatello, Idaho's second-largest city, apparently took its name from that of Pocataro, a Shoshone chief, but it owes its prominence—and a lot of its soul—to railroading. The Utah and Northern narrow-gauge and Oregon Short Line railways, both part of the Union Pacific system, intersected at Pocatello, and railroad activity spurred settlement and construction. By World War II, more than 4,500 railroad cars passed through Pocatello each day. Rail fans may want to pay a visit to the old **Oregon Short Line Depot** on West Bonneville Street. President William Taft attended the dedication of this building, erected in 1915. The Yellowstone Hotel, frequently used by rail passengers, is just across the street from the old depot. These days it is home to **The Golden Wheel,** a locally popular restaurant. Pocatello still has passenger rail service via Amtrak; the station is at 300 South Harrison Avenue.

Perhaps because of its railroad links, perhaps because it is home to a university, Pocatello has a different feel than Idaho's other large towns: More transient, a bit scruffy, but not without a charm of its own. There are definitely a few spots worth checking out, notably the ◈ **Continental Bistro** at 140 South Main. On a warm day it's possible to peer through the Bistro's windows and see the place look abandoned. But that's because most patrons favor the restaurant's spacious rear patio, bedecked with flowers and bordered by exposed brick walls covered with ivy. At lunchtime the Bistro offers a good variety of salads, sandwiches, and pasta dishes, most in the $4.25 to $6.50 price range. A crab Mornay sandwich features Canadian crab and gratinéed Swiss cheese served on open-face sourdough bread; the Black Forest club is smoked ham, turkey breast, Havarti cheese, lettuce, and tomato on rye bread or a sourdough roll.

At dinner the Bistro is perhaps best known for its Filet du Boeuf, which chef Rob Wiscombe prepares in a different manner each day. Appetizers range in price from $1.95 for onion soup gratinée to $7.95 for escargot glacéed Dijonnaise en croute. Pasta dishes run $8.95 to $10.95, and a good variety of other entrées is available, including veal, lobster, lamb chops, and roast duck. The Continental Bistro also has a lounge featuring sixteen microbrews and import beers on tap, a wine list of about 100 selections, and live jazz and blues each Wednesday night. The Continental Bistro is open for dining from 11:00 A.M. to 10:00 P.M. Monday through Saturday, with the patio generally open May through October. The lounge is open until 1:00 A.M. nightly. For more information or reservations call (208) 233–4433.

After your meal, take a stroll around downtown Pocatello, better known as Old Town these days. For a look around the rest of the city, try the Pocatello Street Car. The hour-long ride through town costs 60 cents and visits such high spots as the Idaho State University campus (with its Idaho Museum of Natural History), the Pine Ridge Mall, and Ross Park. The streetcar route also runs to the ◆ **Standrod House,** one of the most impressive mansions in Idaho. The house, located at 648 North Garfield, was built in 1901 by Judge Drew W. Standrod, and it served for years as the epicenter of Pocatello's artistic, literary, and social life. The home's exterior is of light grey and red sandstone quarried in nearby McCammon and hauled to the site by horse-drawn wagons. Inside, the mansion boasts parquet floors, leaded-glass windows, golden oak, French marble fireplaces and wash basins, and glazed tile. The city of Pocatello acquired and renovated the Standrod House in the 1970s; it is now open for tours and available for private parties. For hours or more information call (208) 234–6184.

Accommodations of a much more modest sort were to be found at Fort Hall, originally situated along the Oregon Trail on what is now the Fort Hall Indian Reservation. But the fort's past is preserved at the ◆ **Fort Hall Replica,** located in Pocatello's Ross Park. First established by Nathaniel Wyeth in 1834 as a fur-trading post, Fort Hall later became an important resting stop for the emigrants. Exhibits at the replica include a blacksmith's shop and extensive displays on Indian lifestyles. A videotape on Fort Hall's history may be viewed on request. The Fort Hall replica is open daily from 9:00 A.M. to 8:00 P.M. from June 1 through Sep-

**Fort Hall Replica**

tember 15, and from 10:00 A.M. to 2:00 P.M. Tuesday through Saturday during April and May. Admission is $1.00 for adults, 50 cents for ages thirteen to eighteen, and 25 cents for ages six through twelve. Ross Park also includes a pool, rose garden, picnic areas, a playground, and a fenced field in which deer and antelope play and elk and bison roam. For more information call (208) 234–1795.

The ◆**Bannock County Historical Museum** is also located in Ross Park. This is a good place to learn more about Pocatello's railroading past; other exhibits include war memorabilia, Indian artifacts, a restored stagecoach, and rooms that offer glimpses into how early Pocatello lived and worked. The museum is open from 10:00 A.M. to 6:00 P.M. daily Memorial Day weekend through Labor Day, and 10:00 A.M. to 2:00 P.M. Tuesday through Saturday the rest of the year. Admission is $1.00 for adults and 50 cents for children ages six to twelve. The phone number is (208) 233–0434.

## HOT BATHS AND PIONEER PATHS

The entire state of Idaho is justly famous for its hot springs. But perhaps no other town has been so blessed with wondrous thermal activity as **Lava Hot Springs,** situated along Highway 30 and the Portneuf River 35 miles southeast of Pocatello.

Tucked in a mile-high mountain valley near the north edge of the Wasatch Range, Lava Hot Springs once served as a winter campground for the Bannock and Shoshone Indian tribes, who thought the local springs held healing powers. Geologists believe the springs have been a consistent 110 degrees for at least fifty million years. The springs are rich with minerals—calcium carbonate, sodium chloride, and magnesium carbonate being most prevalent—but have no sulfur and, therefore, none of the nose-wrinkling odor typical of many hot springs.

The town has two main attractions, both operated by a state-run foundation: an ❖ **Olympic Swimming Complex** on the west side and the ❖ **Lava Hot Pools** on the east end. The huge free-form Olympic pool has one-third of an acre of water surface, 50-meter racing lanes, a 10–meter diving tower, and a surrounding carpet of green grass for sunbathing; another 25-meter pool nearby meets Amateur Athletic Union standards. Both are open Memorial Day through Labor Day, from 10:00 A.M. to 8:00 P.M. Saturdays, and 11:00 A.M. to 8:00 P.M. weekdays and Sundays. The five hot pools—open every day of the year except Thanksgiving and Christmas—are set amid the sunken gardens of an extinct volcano and range in temperature from 104 to 112 degrees. Three are whirlpools: two of them public, one private. Hours at the hot pools are 8:00 A.M. to 11:00 P.M. April through September, and 9:00 A.M. to 10:00 P.M. October through March. A $7.00 fee buys all-day admission to both the pools and the hot baths; single admission to either the pools or the baths runs $4.00 for adults and teens and $3.50 for children and senior citizens. Suits, towels, and lockers may be rented, and group rates are available. Call (800) 423–8597 for more information.

The pools, hot baths, and Portneuf River tubing have made Lava Hot Springs justly popular, so quite a few other tourist-oriented businesses have sprung up to serve visitors. Motel rates are unusually reasonable for a resort area; many rooms (some including private hot mineral baths) go for about $35 a night. The most expensive places in town top out at about $85, the going rate for the Jacuzzi suite at the **Lava Hot Springs Inn,** a European-style bed and breakfast supposedly complete with its own ghost. (The inn's phone number is 208–776–5830.) The **Lazy A Ranch,** located just west of town, offers Old West chuckwagon dinners accompanied by live music and cowboy entertainment at 7:00 P.M. Thursdays through Saturdays. Call (208) 776–5035 for reservations. **Katie's Bread Shed,** a little roadside stand about 6 miles west of town, is also worth a stop if you're lucky enough to find it open.

Lava Hot Springs has a full calendar of summer special events, including a big **Corvette Car Show** the last weekend in June and a mountain man rendezvous and **Pioneer Days** celebration in mid-July. But autumn may be the best time of all to visit; room rates dip even lower at some establishments, and the surrounding hills are ablaze with some of Idaho's most colorful fall foliage. For more information on Lava Hot Springs, call (800) 548–5282.

Heading east from Lava Hot Springs or west from Soda Springs, consider a short side trip to the ghost town of ◆ **Chesterfield.** Most extinct Western towns owed their existence to mining, but Chesterfield had its roots in agriculture. Mormon pioneers settled the town in 1880 along the old Oregon Trail. The town reached its peak in the 1920s with a population of about 500 people. After that, however, Chesterfield slowly shrunk. After World War II, few local boys came home, and the town lost its post office a few years later.

No one lives year-round in Chesterfield today, but the town's memory remains remarkably well preserved. About two dozen buildings still stand, with plans to rebuild a few others. The most notable remaining structure is the old Chesterfield LDS Ward meetinghouse, which the Daughters of Utah Pioneers have preserved as a museum. Daffodils and a manicured lawn greet visitors, while exhibits inside the handsome brick building include photos of many early settlers, an old pump organ, and a tribute to the prolific Western novelist Frank Robertson, a local boy who grew up to write 128 books (including eight each in 1935 and 1936).

The museum may be toured May through October by checking

with the caretaker couple who live nearby at 3111 Moses Lane. (Look for signs giving directions.) Many descendants of early Chesterfield residents come back each Memorial Day for a luncheon and reunion. Nearby Chesterfield Reservoir is a good fishing spot, too. Chesterfield is located 10 miles north of the town of Bancroft and 15 miles north of U.S. Route 30.

Continuing east on Highway 30, the traveler reaches Soda Springs, Caribou County's seat and largest town. The area was another major point along the Oregon Trail, with many emigrants stopping to camp and sample the water from the area's many natural springs. Most are gone now, but evidence remains of two of the most famous.

One pioneer spring is preserved under a small pavilion in **Hooper Springs Park,** located 2 miles north of the center of town. "Drink deeply of nature's best beverage," a plaque advises. Hooper Springs is named for W. H. Hooper, who was a leading Salt Lake City banker, Utah congressman, and president of the Zion's Cooperative Mercantile Institution (still going as ZCMI, one of the Intermountain region's major department store chains). He had a summer home in Soda Springs and helped the town's soda water reach international markets.

Another spring regularly gave off a sound like that of a steamboat. It's now drowned beneath Alexander Reservoir, but **Steamboat Spring** hasn't disappeared altogether; on a clear day, it can still be viewed puffing and percolating beneath the water's surface. The best way to see evidence of the spring is to play a round on the ◆**Oregon Trail Golf Course.** Look south to the reservoir from either the No. 1 green or the No. 8 tee. From those vantage points, you can also see what are probably the only Oregon Trail wagon ruts on a golf course, a phenomenon once featured in *National Geographic.* Traces of the wagons' wheels cut across the No. 9 fairway and skirt the No. 1 green before traveling across the No. 8 fairway. Still another famous local spring tasted almost exactly like beer, with similar effects, but it—unfortunately—has vanished completely.

Three other Soda Springs attractions are of particular note. The town has the world's only captive geyser, the centerpiece of the aptly named ◆**Geyser Park.** The gusher was discovered in 1937 as the town attempted to find a hot-water source for its swimming pool. The drill hit the geyser, which was later capped and

**Geyser Park**

controlled by a timer. These days it erupts every half-hour in the summer and every hour on the hour in the winter (unless strong west winds are blowing, which would send the 150-foot-high spray cascading over nearby businesses). The surrounding park offers a pleasant place to rest while waiting for the next "show."

North of town, The Nature Conservancy has established a preserve at ◆**Formation Springs.** Here visitors see crystal-clear pools amid a wetlands area at the base of the Aspen Mountains. The springs that feed the pools and nearby creek system deposit high concentrations of calcium carbonate, giving the site its unusual geology. Formation Cave, about 20 feet tall and 1,000 feet long, is among the impressive features, and abundant wildlife may be seen.

Also north of town, the Monsanto Chemical Company has produced a **man-made lava flow.** Monsanto, which produces elemental phosphorous—a substance used in laundry detergents, soft drinks, toothpaste, and other products—at its Soda Springs plant, dumps the resulting slag from its electric furnaces. The slag, 1,400 degrees hot, is poured into trucks bearing special cast-steel pots. The trucks then dump the molten rock onto the slag pile five times each hour, twenty-four hours a day. You can almost imagine the local kids asking each other, "Whaddya wanna do tonight, watch MTV, cruise Highway 30, or go to the slag heap?"

## BEAR LAKE COUNTRY

Two designated scenic routes traverse the state's extreme southeastern corner, intersecting in Soda Springs. The **Pioneer Historic Byway** follows state Highway 34 northeast to Wyoming, skirting the shores of Blackfoot Reservoir and Grays Lake, and the south to Preston and Franklin, two of Idaho's oldest towns. The **Bear Lake-Caribou Scenic Byway** follows U.S. Highways 30 and 89 through Montpelier and south to Bear Lake, a 20-mile-long recreational paradise straddling the Idaho-Utah border. We'll look at the region following a clockwise direction southeast from Soda Springs and back north toward Pocatello.

Settled in 1864 by Mormon families, Montpelier was named for the capital of Brigham Young's home state, Vermont. The town is best known for a reenactment each July of the Oregon

Trail pioneers' trek up the "Big Hill" east of town and for an 1896 visit by Butch Cassidy. The famous outlaw was one of three men who robbed the local bank of $7,165. The bank they robbed is gone now, but the building in which it stood remains on Washington Street downtown.

Montpelier's history can be traced at the ❖ **Rails and Trails Museum,** open Memorial Day through Labor Day at 914 Washington Street. The collections include Oregon Trail lore, Indian artifacts, and pioneer and railroad memorabilia, and a new gallery displays the works of area artists. Don't miss the exhibits on Thomas L. "Peg Leg" Smith, a nineteenth-century mountain man who had to amputate his own leg. Smith opened a trading post at what is now Dingle, Idaho, and reportedly made $100 a day catering to the needs of emigrants bound for California and Oregon.

Although southeast Idaho is geographically and politically part of the Gem State, spiritually the region is closely aligned with Utah and Mormonism. Nowhere is this more true than in the towns and counties bordering the Beehive State. In fact, the 1863 settlers who arrived in what was to become Paris, Idaho, thought they were in Utah until an 1872 boundary survey set the record straight.

The imposing and beautiful ❖ **Paris Stake Tabernacle** was a labor of love for the local Mormon settlers, who spent half a decade building the Romanesque-style church, completed in 1889. A "stake" is the term used by the Church of Jesus Christ of Latter-day Saints to describe a geographical area; the Paris, Idaho, stake was the first organized outside the Utah territory, and the tabernacle was built to serve the Mormon communities and congregations that sprung up within a 50-mile radius of the town.

The tabernacle—designed by Joseph Young, a son of Brigham— was built from red sandstone hauled by horse- and ox-drawn wagons from a canyon 18 miles away. In the winter the rock was pulled by sled over frozen Bear Lake. A former shipbuilder crafted the ceiling, using pine harvested in nearby forests. Tours are offered daily through the summer; arrive mid-day and you may be treated to music from the tabernacle's Austin pipe organ.

A monument on the tabernacle grounds honors Charles Coulson Rich, the man sent by Brigham Young to settle the Bear Lake Valley. It was Rich who, on one of his many missions for the church, went to Europe to find the skilled craftsmen recruited by the Mormons to help build their new churches and towns in the

**97**

American West. Rich had six wives and fifty children and ulti-mately became an apostle in his church. Despite his contribu-tions, Paris was named not for Rich but for Frederick Perris, who platted the townsite. One of the first **settler cabins,** built in 1863 by Thomas Sleight and Charles Atkins, is still standing and may be seen in a park near the tabernacle.

Several intriguing side canyons south of Paris beckon independent-minded motorists from well-traveled Highway 89. **Bloomington Canyon,** west of the tiny town of the same name, leads to a pristine little lake and meadows filled with wildflowers. ◆**Minnetonka Cave,** located west of St. Charles, is the largest developed limestone cave in Idaho and among the state's more spectacular underground wonderlands. Ninety-minute tours weave through a half-mile of fantastic formations and fossils of preserved tropical plant and marine life in nine separate chambers, the largest of which is about 300 feet around and 90 feet high.

In the late 1930s, the federal government began development of Minnetonka Cave via the Works Progress Administration, con-structing a trail from St. Charles Canyon and installing interior paths, steps, and railings. But the cave was only open for a couple of years before World War II began, halting efforts at improvement. After the war the Paris Lions Club operated the cave for a time. It is now managed by the U.S. Forest Service as part of the Cache National Forest. Tours of Minnetonka Cave are given every half-hour from 10:30 A.M. to 5:00 P.M. each day from mid-June through Labor Day. Visitors should be prepared for lots of steps and cool temperatures; good walking shoes and a jacket are recommended. Several campgrounds are available up St. Charles Canyon. For more information on the cave or surrounding forest, call (208) 847–0375.

St. Charles serves as gateway to ◆**Bear Lake,** one of the bluest bodies of water in North America. Explanations for its turquoise tint vary, but it's usually credited to a high concentra-tion of soluble carbonates. Photographers find the lake at its most beautiful at sunrise, when the water frequently glints pink, red, and gold as it catches the waking orb's rays. But sunset visitors are more likely to spy the Bear Lake Monster. Rumors of the beast have circulated for centuries, first by Native Americans and mountain men, later by Joseph Rich (a son of Mormon pioneer Charles Coulson Rich), who reported his findings in an 1868 article for the *Deseret News* of Salt Lake City.

Bear Lake is also unique because it boasts several species of fish found nowhere else. In addition to the rainbow and cutthroat trout so plentiful throughout the Rockies, Bear Lake is home to the Bonneville cisco, a sardinelike whitefish that spawns each January and is popular year-round for bait. Check with the Idaho Department of Fish and Game at (800) 635–7820 for regulations on angling for cisco or other fish; information and licenses are also available at sporting goods dealers throughout the state.

In addition to fish, Bear Lake Country is thick with animals and birds. The ◆ **Bear Lake National Wildlife Refuge** at the lake's north end draws Canada geese; sandhill and whooping cranes; redhead, canvasback, and mallard ducks; and the nation's largest nesting population of white-face ibis. Deer, moose, and smaller mammals are also known to wander through the refuge's nearly 18,000 acres. Check with the refuge office in Montpelier or call (208) 847–1757 for information on waterfowl hunting, boating, and hiking opportunities.

Our explorations of Southeastern Idaho continue at Franklin, the state's oldest town. Franklin, founded in 1860, beats out Paris for the title of Idaho's oldest town by three years. But like the settlers of Paris, Franklin's early townsfolk thought they were Utahns until the 1872 survey confirmed the town's location in what was to become the state of Idaho.

Franklin's museum is called **The Relic Hall,** and it houses many artifacts and photos of pioneer life. A park complete with picnic grounds and a fireplace now surrounds the hall. Two of Franklin's most interesting sights are located just outside of town on the Old Yellowstone Highway. (Turn west at the Daughters of the Utah Pioneers marker north of town.) The ruins on the north side of the road are those of what is likely the **oldest flour mill** in the state of Idaho. And just across the road, the **Yellowstone Rock** shows the old route to the nation's first national park. After Yellowstone received its national park designation, large boulders with arrows pointing the way were placed along what was then the main road to the park to help travelers find their way. This may be the last such marker still in existence.

The scenic Cub River Canyon east of Highway 91 between Franklin and Preston is home to the ◆ **Deer Cliff Inn,** which bills itself as "The Most Romantic Spot in the West." Family-run

**99**

since 1940, this rustic retreat offers cabins and a restaurant featuring summer streamside patio dining. Menu items range from $6.75 to $16.25 and include steaks, chicken, shrimp, trout, halibut, and lobster. The restaurant is open from 5:00 P.M. Monday through Saturday during June, July, and August, and from 5:00 P.M. Thursday through Saturday during May, September, and October (except on holidays May through September, when it opens at noon). Live entertainment is on hand most Friday and Saturday nights. For more information call (208) 852–0643.

Brigham Young, the Mormon leader, urged his followers to heed the golden rule when dealing with Native Americans. "Treat them in all respects as you would like to be treated," he said in an 1852 speech. Indeed, the Mormons who settled Idaho early on made pacts with the local Indian chiefs to share crops and live together peaceably. Still there were tensions, and they boiled over in January 1863 in the **Battle of Bear River** 2.5 miles north of Preston. More Indians died in this little-known incident than in any other; there were more casualties—as many as 400 men, women, and children killed—than at Wounded Knee, Sand Creek, or Little Big Horn.

The battle was triggered by the death of a miner on Bear River during an Indian attack; Colonel Patrick Connor of the Third California Infantry, stationed at Fort Douglas near Salt Lake City, used the incident as an excuse to make war. William Hull, a local pioneer who witnessed the battle, gave this account of its aftermath: "Never will I forget the scene, dead bodies were everywhere. I counted eight deep in one place and in several places they were three to five deep. In all we counted nearly 400; two-thirds of this number being women and children." A monument along the east side of Highway 91 north of Preston makes note of the battle, and the actual battle site was nearby along aptly named Battle Creek.

Malad City, the seat of Oneida County, is more on the beaten path (Interstate 15) than off, but it has a few spots to recommend a stop. The ◆**Iron Door Playhouse** offers a full theatrical menu of about ten productions each year including Broadway fare, youth-oriented shows, dinner theater, cowboy poetry, and melodramas. The playhouse is located at 59 North Main Street in what was once one of the nation's first J.C. Penney stores, since remodeled into a modern theater. Call (208) 766–4705 or (208)

766–4014 for reservations or information on upcoming events.

And what about that "Iron Door" name? "Malad" is French for "sick," and—like the Malad Gorge and Malad River in South Central Idaho—Malad City and its nearby (and much longer) Malad River reportedly earned their names when a party of trappers became sick after drinking from the stream. But those early trappers probably didn't feel nearly as sick as did Glispie Waldron, who, in 1890, may have blown his chance at finding a buried treasure.

It seems that during the 1860s and 1870s, Malad City was a major stop for freight wagons taking supplies from Utah north to the mines of Idaho and Montana, as well as those returning with gold. This traffic also made Malad a favorite target of robbers and other ne'er-do-wells, one group of which reportedly hid the loot from a stagecoach hold-up somewhere in the Samaria Mountains located southwest of town, planning to retrieve it later. Waldron was traveling in the area in 1890 when he reportedly spied an iron door covering a cave. He tied his coat to a nearby tree to mark the spot, intending to return. But he didn't make it back for a couple of years, and by then, his coat was gone. To this day, treasure seekers are still searching for the fabled iron door and the riches that may lie behind it. If you're interested in trying your own luck, stop by the **Pioneer Museum** at 27 Bannock Street in Malad City for tips on where to look.

If you haven't had your fill of Southeastern Idaho water recreation by now, check out ❖ **Downata Hot Springs Resort,** located near the town of Downey. Aside from a pool and water slides, this year-round resort offers everything from RV and tent camping to calf roping. Downey is on Highway 91, 6 miles south of its junction with Interstate 15. Call (208) 897–5736 for more information.

# EASTERN IDAHO

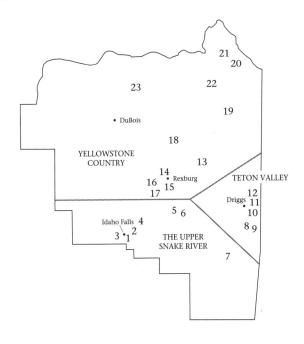

21
20
22
23
19
• DuBois
18
YELLOWSTONE
COUNTRY
13
TETON VALLEY
14
16 • Rexburg
15
17
12
Driggs 11
10
5 6
Idaho Falls 4
8 9
3 •1 2
THE UPPER
SNAKE RIVER
7

1. Idaho Falls Greenbelt
2. Bonneville County Historical Museum
3. Reed's Dairy
4. Country Store Boutique
5. Mountain River Ranch
6. Cress Creek Nature Trail
7. The Lodge at Palisades Creek
8. Pierre's Playhouse
9. Victor Steak Bank
10. Pines Motel Guest Haus
11. Grand Targhee Ski & Summer Resort
12. Spud Drive-In
13. Teton Dam Site
14. Teton Flood Museum
15. Idaho Centennial Carousel
16. Menan Buttes
17. Jefferson County TV & Pioneer Museum
18. St. Anthony Sand Dunes
19. Upper Mesa Falls
20. Big Springs
21. Jacobs' Island Park Ranch
22. Railroad Ranch
23. Spencer Opal Mine

# Eastern Idaho
## The Upper Snake River

In Eastern Idaho the outdoors are never far away. This is the western gateway to two of America's premiere national parks, as well as to swift-running rivers and backcountry byways. Mountain peaks rim every horizon, shadowing the fertile, irrigated fields. Even within the city limits of the region's biggest town, Idaho Falls, nature makes her presence known.

Unlike Twin Falls, where a set of Snake River cascades gave the town its name, Idaho Falls got its name before any falls really existed. The city started life as Eagle Rock, taking that name from a ferry built in 1863 by Bill Hickman and Harry Rickards. (The ferry was positioned near a small rock island on which bald eagles frequently nested in a juniper tree.) In its early days Eagle Rock served as a major fording point for miners heading to the riches of central and western Idaho; the community was also known as Taylor's Crossing or Taylor's Bridge for the early span built by James "Matt" Taylor. Later, Eagle Rock served as the center of railroad activity in the new Idaho Territory, but all that changed in 1887 when the Union Pacific moved its headquarters south to Pocatello and Eagle Rock's population plummeted. By 1891, a team of Chicago developers—Charles N. Lee, W. G. Emerson, D. W. Higbee, J. B. Holmes, and Bernard McCaffery—had descended on Eagle Rock. Seeing the rapids on the Snake River, they encouraged the locals to change the town's name to Idaho Falls. But it wasn't until 1911 that man-made falls were completed, giving the city legitimate claim to its name.

Since then Idaho Falls has made good use of its riverside location. The 2.5-mile ◆**Idaho Falls Greenbelt** runs between the falls area and downtown, offering office and shop workers a pleasant place to spend the lunch hour. On weekends, local residents flock to the greenbelt to enjoy a picnic, often sharing their food with the numerous ducks and geese who call the area home. Joggers, cyclists, strollers, and in-line skaters also enjoy the greenbelt's picturesque view. **Penny's Deli** at 376 Shoup Avenue will pack a sack lunch for you to take to the greenbelt, and the **Wheat Blossom Bakery** at 445 "A" Street is known to give out free bread for feeding the ducks (as well as free samples of their other goodies for human consumption). Altogether, Idaho Falls has forty parks; another of the most notable is Tautphaus Park, home of the **Idaho Falls Zoo.** Exhibits include a cat complex with three species of big cats, a bi-level otter exhibit, regular-size zebras and miniature "zebus," pot-bellied pigs, monkeys, and more. The zoo is open summer days from 10:00 A.M. to 8:00 P.M.; for more information call (208) 529–1480.

Idaho Falls also boasts an abundance of interesting architecture. The city's landmark structure is the **Idaho Falls Temple** of the Church of Jesus Christ of Latter-day Saints, located along the Snake River at 1000 Memorial Drive, its spire visible for miles. The temple's visitors center is open daily from 9:00 A.M. to 9:00 P.M. Free tours are available, and exhibits highlight Mormon history, art, and culture.

Elsewhere in the city, the Idaho Falls Historic Preservation Committee has prepared several informative pamphlets detailing walking tours. For example, the **Ridge Avenue Historic District** has sixty-seven notable buildings, with styles ranging from Queen Anne to craftsman to colonial revival. One of the most auspicious structures on the tour is the First Presbyterian Church at 325 Elm Street, a neoclassical building complete with Roman dome and Ionic portico. History buffs will enjoy a stop at the ◆ **Bonneville County Historical Museum,** located at 200 North Eastern Avenue in a former Carnegie library. After passing through the museum's art deco entrance, visitors are treated to exhibits ranging from pioneer life to the atomic age, along with a replica of the original Eagle Rock town site. The museum is open from 10:00 A.M. to 5:00 P.M. Monday through Friday, and 1:00 to 5:00 P.M. Saturdays; closed Sundays and holidays. Admission is $1.00, or 25 cents for children under eighteen. Guided tours are available; for more information call (208) 522–1400.

You've probably heard of Ben & Jerry's, but have you heard of Al & Reed's? This premium, all-natural ice cream is made at ◆ **Reed's Dairy,** located on the western outskirts of Idaho Falls at 2660 West Broadway (just west of Broadway and Bellin, on the north side). Al & Reed's ice cream is unique because it's made with Idaho potatoes and sweetened with fruit. The result is a dessert with half the calories and a fraction of the fat found in most premium ice creams. Reed's also makes traditional ice cream, about forty flavors in all. Visitors to the dairy's on-the-

**Reed's Dairy**

premises store usually have their pick of eighteen varieties, including three made with potatoes. Cones, shakes, sundaes, frozen yogurt, and sandwiches are available; there is informal seating inside and out; and tours are offered, too. Reed's Dairy is open from 8:00 A.M. to 10:00 P.M. in the summer and until 9:00 P.M. the rest of the year. For more information phone (208) 522–0123.

Highway 26, the road from Idaho Falls to Grand Teton National Park, isn't exactly off the beaten path. Sometimes in our hurry to get somewhere else, however, we miss seeing something interesting right along our way. Such is the case with the big, unusual looking building at 4523 Highway 26, a few miles north of Idaho Falls. For years I drove by wondering: Was it a school? A barn? Actually, it was both: a school built in 1899 and a barn erected shortly thereafter. Both structures now sit on the same site and serve as home to the ✦ **Country Store Boutique,** a fascinating antiques and gift emporium run by Mary and Lock Seneff, their son Eric, and his wife, Melanie.

The Country Store Boutique boasts 15,000 square feet of the old, new, and unusual. Unlike many shops featuring antiques and collectibles, the Country Store Boutique doesn't feel musty and overstuffed. There's room to move around amid the solid old wood furniture, the antique glassware, the one-of-a-kind dresses, and the Indian pottery and jewelry. The boutique also carries quilts, rugs, baskets, arrowheads, sheet music, folk art, and more. It's a great place to shop for a gift or for your home. The store is open from 10:00 A.M. to 6:00 P.M. Monday through Saturday. Call (208) 522–8450 for more information.

East of Idaho Falls in Ririe, **Heise Hot Springs** features a 95-degree swimming pool with water slide and a soothing 105-degree mineral hot bath. But this popular resort doesn't stop there; visitors can also camp amid tall cottonwood trees, tee off on a nine-hole par 29 golf course, grab a bite at the pizza parlor, or spread a picnic on the lawn. Heise Hot Springs is open year-round, with swimming from 10:00 A.M. to 10:00 P.M. For more information call (208) 538–7312.

◆**Mountain River Ranch,** also near Ririe, is another spot offering a wide variety of entertainment and recreation. In summertime covered wagons transport visitors to the Meadow Muffin Theatre, where Western variety shows and melodramas are presented as guests munch on a chuck-wagon dinner of barbecued chicken, potato salad, baked beans, corn on the cob, watermelon, and lemonade. In wintertime sleigh rides run nearly nightly in December and weekends through February, and shows and dinners are still on the menu, too. In addition the ranch offers a fee-fishing trout pond (no license required), an RV park, trailers for rent on-site, tent camping, weekend trail rides, and a restaurant. For more information call (208) 538–7337, or write to Mountain River Ranch, 98 North 5050 East, Ririe 83443.

The ◆**Cress Creek Nature Trail** is yet another worthy stop east of Ririe off the Heise Road. This well-marked path gives visitors a chance to learn about the flora, fauna, and geology of Eastern Idaho, all while enjoying some tremendous views. At one point the panorama stretches from the Caribou Mountain Range south of the Snake River all the way to the Beaverhead Range on the Montana border. The Blackfoot Mountains, Big Southern

Butte and East Twin Butte, the Lost River Mountain Range, and the Menan Buttes may all be seen as well.

U.S. Highway 26 continues to follow the Upper Snake River toward its origin in Wyoming. The Swan Valley-Palisades area is one of Eastern Idaho's least populated and most scenic stretches. Several U.S. Forest Service campgrounds along **Palisades Reservoir** provide excellent bases for enjoying the region's good fishing and boating.

Indoor accommodations are available, too. **McBride's Bed & Breakfast** offers its patrons a separate, 900-square-foot guest house with a king bed, queen bed, and two twin beds, plus a coffee pot, refrigerator, and television. Guests can either grill their dinner in the backyard or eat at a local cafe. In the morning, innkeeper Deanna McBride offers a full country breakfast, served whenever the guests wish. Wildlife is abundant, with bald eagles, elk, deer, moose, and beaver all living nearby. The McBride's guest house can accommodate up to six people, with children under age six staying free. Rates run from $33 for one person to $85 for six people per night. For more information call (208) 483–4221, or write to Deanna McBride, P.O. Box 166, Irwin 83428.

❖ **The Lodge at Palisades Creek** is an even more luxurious option. This rustic-yet-elegant resort sits within casting distance of the Snake River, and the fly-fishing is so good that dinner is served until 10:00 P.M. to accommodate guests who wish to stay in the river well into the evening. The Lodge is pricey—$340 per person, per night, double occupancy with a three-day minimum stay required in July and August—but the rate includes guide service, accommodations, and gourmet meals. (Rates are less for nonanglers: Weeklong packages, overnight trips, and guide service without accommodations are available, too.) For more information call (208) 483–2222, or write The Lodge at Palisades Creek, P.O. Box 70, Irwin 83428.

At Swan Valley, the traveler has a choice: Continue on Highway 26 to Alpine, Wyoming, or take Idaho State Highway 31 over Pine Creek Pass, elevation 6,764. The latter provides access to Idaho's Teton Valley, the area we will explore next.

## TETON VALLEY

Wyoming's Teton Range ranks among the world's most magnificent chains of mountains. The classic view of the Tetons is from the east, but Idaho's Teton Valley offers a less-crowded, equally scenic approach to the famed peaks. In fact, State Highways 31, 33, and 32 (in that order, from south to north) have been designated Idaho's **Teton Scenic Byway.** Along the way the drive winds through several small towns—Victor, Driggs, and Tetonia—oriented to outdoor recreation.

Mostly outdoor, anyway. There are a few indoor diversions that make the Teton Valley a most worthy day-trip or weekend destination. ◆ **Pierre's Playhouse,** going strong into its fourth decade, presents 1890s-style melodramas mid-June through the Saturday before Labor Day at its theater on Main Street in Victor. Each show is preceded by a delicious Dutch oven dinner featuring chicken, potatoes, a scone, and coffee. While waiting for your food, you can always amuse yourself by reading the rules and regulations on the playbill; these include "Children left in the theatre over three days become the property of the villain," "Firearms may not be discharged in the direction of the stage," and "It is requested that liquor not be imported into the theatre in any other than a human container."

Proprietress Peggy Egbert plays the piano and presides over the merriment. She started the playhouse with her husband, Tom, in the early 1960s. Tom has passed away, but Peggy still runs the show, which attracts about a quarter of its audience from outside Idaho each summer. Cost is $13.00 for the show and dinner, or $7.00 for just the show. Dinner is served from 6:00 P.M. on, with the curtain at 8:00 P.M. Reservations are advised; call (208) 787–2249.

The ◆ **Victor Steak Bank** may be a restaurant today, but that's only the most recent of the building's many incarnations. The cafe once was a mercantile, later converted to a bank by B. F. Blodgett. When the local school burned, it became a school and community center where folks would meet for everything from dances to elections. When a new school was completed, the building became a honky-tonk; later still, it was used as a bus garage, then the Victor city repair shop, and then the fire station.

The Steak Bank remains a popular gathering spot, especially at breakfast, when local farmers, ranchers, and other residents sit around as long as they can spare to drink coffee, talk about irrigation pumps, and compare golf scores. A sign on the wall posts the "coffee rules—fifty cents for one hour, $2.00 all day, ask about our weekly rates." The menu's fare is basic and hearty, with sourdough cakes, homemade soups, and sandwiches topping the bill. When it comes time to pay, you do so at an old-fashioned cashier's cage, where you are encouraged to "make deposits regularly." Victor Steak Bank is located at 13 South Main near the junction of Highways 31 and 33, and it's open from 5:30 A.M. to 10:00 P.M. For more information call (208) 787–2277.

If you prefer lighter fare, **Table Rock Cafe** at 285 North Main in Driggs may be the spot for you. This friendly place has an eclectic menu that features the cafe's own fresh-baked goods, espresso, and a variety of served-all-day items including Kokopelli Chili, Big Hole Nachos, Hummus in Pita, a Halibut Burger, plus daily specials. If you're feeling a bit tuckered out from a long drive or a day of outdoor fun, try a fruit-juice smoothie, perhaps stoked up by a bit of wheat germ, ginseng, protein powder, or bee pollen. Table Rock Cafe is open from 8 A.M. to 6 P.M. daily except Sundays. Call (208) 354–8663 for more information.

The ◆ **Pines Motel Guest Haus** at 105 South Main in Driggs is an unusual combination of mom-and-pop motel, bed-and-breakfast inn, and community social center. Originally a two-story log cabin built about 1900, the building has been enlarged and is now home to John and Nancy Nielson and their family. Many travelers who stay at the Pines Motel Guest Haus seem to wind up part of the Nielson's extended clan, returning for holiday dinners and corresponding with the family. Outdoors, a stone fireplace, gas grill, lawn chairs, and play area offer summertime fun and relaxation. Local people and tourists alike turn out for Driggs's annual antiques show, held in the Nielsons' backyard each Fourth of July, and for ice skating on the pond John builds each winter. Visitors needn't worry about bringing their own skates; the Nielsons have a collection with enough pairs to fit nearly anyone.

The Pines Motel Guest Haus has eight rooms ranging in price from $35 to $50 double occupancy. Children and pets are welcome. The Nielsons serve a big country-style breakfast on antique dishes in one of the original log-cabin rooms. The meal is included in the price of two bed-and-breakfast rooms with a shared bath and is $8.00 extra per person for guests in the other rooms (half-price for children twelve and under). For more information or reservations, call (208) 354–2774, or write the Pines Motel Guest Haus, P.O. Box 117, Driggs 83422.

Driggs also is the jumping-off spot for ◆ **Grand Targhee Ski & Summer Resort,** just over the border in Alta, Wyoming, and accessible only via the Tetons' Idaho side. Targhee is well known for getting a pile of snow, typically more than 500 inches each winter, including plenty of powder. For several years running, readers of *Snow Country* magazine have ranked Grand Targhee number one nationally in snow-condition report accuracy. With that in mind, the resort has introduced a snow guarantee—anyone who finds snow conditions unsatisfactory may turn their lift ticket in by 11:00 A.M. and receive a voucher good for any other day during the current ski season. Targhee is also a target of extreme skiers, with several instructional workshops typically planned each winter.

But Grand Targhee is worth a visit in warmer weather, too. The resort is the site for several annual summer events, including three summer music festivals. The **Rockin' the Tetons Music Festival** usually takes place in mid-July, followed by Michael Martin Murphey's **WestFest** in late July, and the **Targhee Bluegrass Festival** in mid-August. (Call for current dates.) There's also good mountain biking, horseback riding, tennis, hiking, and a climbing wall, plus activities and child care for kids of all ages. Resort staff will even arrange a fly-fishing, river rafting, or soaring expedition nearby. For more information on Grand Targhee, call (800) TARGHEE, or write to Grand Targhee Resort, Box Ski, Alta, WY 83422.

Drive-in movie theaters are dying out across much of North America, but there remain a fair number in the Gem State, including one in the little town of Driggs. And appropriately enough for Idaho, this one's called the ◆ **Spud Drive-In.** Located just south of town, the drive-in's giant potato is a landmark throughout the region, and its hamburgers are pretty famous, too. For twenty-four-hour movie information, call (208) 354–2727.

## YELLOWSTONE COUNTRY

Just west of Tetonia the Teton Scenic Byway continues north on State Highway 32, terminating in Ashton (where the Mesa Falls Scenic Byway begins; see below). Highway 33 continues west to Rexburg, largest city in the Teton Valley. En route plan a stop at the ◆ **Teton Dam Site,** just a mile and a half north of Highway

**111**

33 near Newdale. A big pyramid of earth is all that is left of the Teton Dam, which collapsed June 5, 1976, killing eleven people and causing nearly $1 billion in damage. (The nearby Idaho state highway historical marker erroneously puts the death toll at fourteen.) The dam—widely opposed by environmentalists—had just been completed and its reservoir was still being filled when the breach occurred, unleashing eighty billion gallons of water toward Wilford, Sugar City, Rexburg, and Idaho Falls. Fortunately most Teton Valley residents heard about the coming torrent and were able to evacuate before the waters swept through their towns.

The ✦ **Teton Flood Museum,** at 51 North Center Street in Rexburg, tells the tale in exhibits, photos, and a fascinating video, *One Saturday Morning.* (Ask at the front desk to view the tape.) Other displays at the museum showcase handmade quilts and a collection of more than 300 salt-and-pepper shakers. The Teton Flood Museum is open from 10:00 A.M. to 5:00 P.M. Monday through Saturday from May through September, and 11:00 A.M. to 4:00 P.M. Monday through Friday the rest of the year. Admission is by donation. For more information phone (208) 356–9101.

While in Rexburg, don't miss the ✦ **Idaho Centennial Carousel,** located in Porter Park. The merry-go-round was built in 1926 by the Spillman Engineering Company of North Tonawanda, New York, and brought to Rexburg in 1952. By the late seventies, the old carousel had been severely damaged by vandalism and the Teton Dam floodwaters. Now, however, the carousel is completely restored and truly one of a kind. Sherrell Anderson, a master carver, replaced more than fifty broken legs and ten tails for the carousel's horses, then created twelve new horses that match the originals in style but are festooned with symbols of Idaho.

The lead horse, "Centennial," is decorated with the state tree (white pine), the state bird (mountain bluebird), the state flower (syringa), the state gemstone (star garnet), and the state seal. On the opposite side, the "Chief Joseph" horse is a grey Appaloosa (Idaho's state horse) fitted with ornamentation including a bear-claw necklace and a shield bearing the portrait of the great Nez Perce leader. The carousel's center is also decorated with pictures and symbols from all over the Gem State, including scenes of Hells Canyon, Balanced Rock, and Harriman State Park, as well as a moose, grizzly bear, and white-tailed deer. The Idaho Centen-

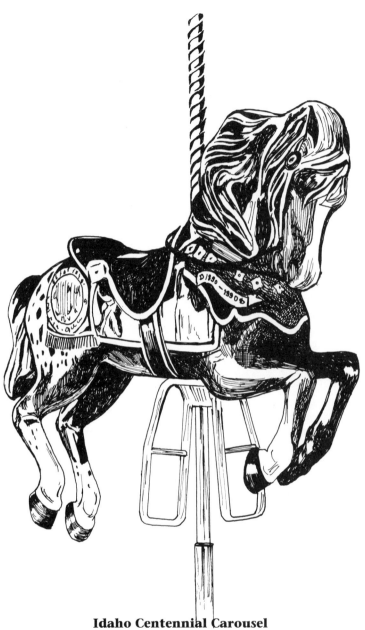

**Idaho Centennial Carousel**

nial Carousel is open for rides from 1:00 to 9:00 P.M. Monday through Saturday during the summer months (except on days with bad weather). It can be reserved for group use; for more information call (208) 359–3020.

The ✦**Menan Buttes,** rising southwest of Rexburg, are another National Natural Landmark and a fun spot for even the littlest hikers (although steep and challenging treks are available for those who want more adventure). The two 10,000-year-old buttes are composed of glassy basalt lava, found in only a few places in the world. The buttes are 800 and 500 feet high, with craters that measure a half-mile wide and about 300 feet deep. The buttes are north of the small town of Menan, or they may be reached by taking State Highway 33 west of Rexburg.

Do you watch television? If so, you may want to make a pilgrimage to Rigby, hometown of **Philo T. Farnsworth,** who invented the cathode-ray tube and made TV possible. No couch potato, Farnsworth was a natural whiz at all things mechanical.

Born in Utah in 1906, he moved to a farm near Rigby when he was a boy. Fascinated by electricity, he played violin in a dance orchestra to earn money for books on the topic. Farnsworth was fourteen years old when he got the idea for TV while plowing a field, and one day he sketched out his ideas on a blackboard at Rigby High School. By 1927 Farnsworth—then living in California—was able to prove his idea worked by transmitting a single horizontal line from a camera in one room to a receiving screen in another. He was just twenty-one.

In 1930 electronics giant RCA offered to buy Farnsworth's invention for a cool $200,000 and give him a job, but the inventor—preferring to preserve his independence—turned them down flat. That refusal apparently triggered the patent war between Farnsworth and RCA, which claimed one of its own employees, Vladimir Zworykin, had actually invented television. Zworykin had been tinkering with TV, but it wasn't until he visited Farnsworth's lab and saw the Idaho native's invention that he was able to duplicate Philo's principles and work. RCA eventually filed suit against Farnsworth, but the inventor prevailed, especially after his former high-school science teacher produced a 1922 sketch of Philo's television theory.

Farnsworth never finished high school, yet by the time he died in 1971 he had earned 300 patents and an honorary doctorate from Brigham Young University. His other notable inventions included the baby incubator, and at the time of his death, he was working on the theory of nuclear fission. Zworykin still sometimes gets credit for Farnsworth's television invention, but the truth is coming out—and someday, Farnsworth's name may be as famous as those of fellow inventors Thomas Edison and Alexander Graham Bell.

The ◆Jefferson County TV and Pioneer Museum has extensive displays about Farnsworth's life and work, including several handwritten journals, his Dictaphone, a Farnsworth television, much of his science book collection, and copies of just about anything ever written about the inventor. Other exhibits detail the early history of Jefferson County and its communities. Museum hours are from 1:00 to 5:00 P.M. Tuesday through Saturday, except Wednesdays, when visitors are welcome until 8:00 P.M. Suggested donation is $1.00 for adults and 25 cents for children. The museum is at 118 West First South in Rigby; just look for the high tower. The phone number is (208) 745–8423.

From Rigby continue northeast on U.S. Highway 20 to St. Anthony, famous for the sand dunes north of town. Like the dunes at Bruneau in Southwestern Idaho, the ◆St. Anthony Sand Dunes are among the highest in the United States, but the St. Anthony complex is much larger than that at Bruneau—about 150 square miles total. The St. Anthony Dunes are particularly popular with all-terrain vehicle enthusiasts. Small, rolling hills are suitable for beginners, and hills up to 500 feet in height offer challenges for more experienced riders. But because the dunes are under consideration for wilderness designation—and because sagebrush and other vegetation at the site provide critical habitat for deer, elk, and sage grouse—visitors must ride on the open sand only. For more information call the Bureau of Land Management (which oversees the dunes) at (208) 524–7500.

Ashton, another 15 miles or so east on Highway 20, is the gateway to the **Mesa Falls Scenic Byway** (Highway 47), a beautiful 25-mile route that runs right by the viewpoints for Lower and Upper Mesa Falls and offers good views of the Teton Range, too. This is one scenic drive that barely takes longer than the more direct highway route, so by all means indulge.

At **Lower Mesa Falls,** an overlook appropriately dubbed Grandview provides a panorama featuring the Henry's Fork of the Snake

**115**

River and the 65-foot falls, which are seen at some distance. Camping and picnicking are available nearby. ◆ **Upper Mesa Falls,** on the other hand, are viewed up close and personal. By descending a series of walkways, it's possible to stand right at the brink of the 114-foot Upper Falls, bask in its thunderous roar, and probably see a rainbow. Benches offer the traveler an opportunity to sit and reflect on the falls and the tall pines all around. Big Falls Inn at Upper Mesa Falls was constructed around the turn of the century and used by travelers en route to Yellowstone National Park. It's now being rehabilitated as a visitor information center. From Upper Mesa Falls the byway continues 12 miles to U.S. Highway 20, returning to the main route near Island Park.

A side trip from the Mesa Falls Scenic Byway takes travelers into the little-known Bechler Meadows area straddling the Idaho-Wyoming border within **Yellowstone National Park.** To take this detour (about 40 miles round-trip), watch 4 miles outside Marysville (itself just east of Ashton) for the Cave Falls Road (1400 North). A campground and ranger station sit nearly smack-dab on the state line at Bechler Meadows. Nearby, a picnic area affords a view of Cave Falls, which drop along the entire width of Falls River. An easy 1-mile trail leads through the pine forest to Bechler Falls.

Island Park is among Idaho's top recreation areas. Aside from being a town of some 200 people, Island Park is a geological feature—a **caldera,** or volcanic basin, the world's largest at about 20 miles in diameter. The caldera was created when a volcano originally situated in the area erupted continuously for thousands of years before finally collapsing. This is also the land of the Henry's Fork, considered one of America's premier trout streams. The river was named for Andrew Henry, who passed through the area in 1810 as part of a fur-trapping expedition and established a trading post. These days numerous outfitters offer guide services and equipment for anglers, snowmobilers, and other recreationists.

◆ **Big Springs,** located northeast of Island Park, is the source of much of the Henry's Fork flow and the home of some truly impressive rainbow trout. A National Natural Landmark, the springs are one of a kind, issuing at the rate of 92,000 gallons per minute from the same rhyolitic lava flows that created the caldera. The Targhee National Forest has a campground at the site. No fishing is allowed at Big Springs, but the trout will happily accept handouts of bread tossed by visitors. The **John Sack**

**Cabin,** listed on the National Register of Historic Places, sits nearby and is open to visitors during the summer.

The Island Park area has several guest ranches. One such spot, ◆ **Jacobs' Island Park Ranch,** is an authentic, working cattle spread. Visitors can watch cowboys on the job, or even help out on a cattle drive. Many guests, however, prefer to play, and the ranch offers horseback riding, boat tours of Island Park Reservoir, fishing, swimming, and nighttime entertainment by Western musicians. In wintertime cross-country skiing and snowmobiling are available. For more information call (208) 662–5567, or write Jacobs' Island Park Ranch, 2496 North 2375 East, Hamer 83425.

**Mack's Inn Resort,** on the banks of the Henry's Fork between Island Park and West Yellowstone, Montana, is another spot Idaho families have enjoyed for generations. The resort sports a variety of accommodations ranging from cabins of several sizes to condos, along with an RV park. Recreational amenities include float trips, paddleboats, miniature golf, basketball, volleyball, horseshoe pits, and more. Phone (208) 558–7272 for more information, or write Mack's Inn Resort, P.O. Box 10, Mack's Inn 83433.

Island Park can be a noisy place in winter, what with all the snowmobilers racing across the white fields of snow. But solace isn't hard to find for those seeking a more serene wintertime experience. **Harriman State Park** has some of the state's best cross-country skiing, and the park is closed to snow machines. That's largely because the park is also a wildlife refuge, home to bald eagles, trumpeter swans, sandhill cranes, elk, deer, moose, and coyotes. Skiers and snowshoers are likely to catch glimpses of these and other animals during any winter trip through the park.

Harriman is peaceful in summertime, too. Trails ranging in length from 1 mile to 5½ miles meander along the Henry's Fork, Silver Lake, and Golden Lake, or up to the top of a ridge where the Teton Range may be viewed. Again these paths are open only to nonmotorized use by hikers, mountain bicyclists, and horseback riders. Visitors may bring their own horse or rent one in the park.

Harriman State Park is also home to the ◆ **Railroad Ranch,** a collection of buildings erected in the early twentieth century by investors from the Oregon Shortline Railroad. Over time the ranch became a favorite retreat of prominent American industrialists and their families. It was E. H. Harriman, founder of the Union Pacific Railroad, who envisioned the ranch as a refuge for wildlife. Ironically, he never really got to enjoy the ranch, but his son and daughter-in-law, E. Roland and Gladys Harriman, spent six weeks of most summers at the ranch, and a cabin remains furnished much as they used it.

Over a half-century, about forty buildings were constructed at the Railroad Ranch. Twenty-seven of these original structures still stand, and many are included in tours given during the summer months. No camping is available in the park, but groups can reserve a bunkhouse that can sleep between fifteen and forty people. The dorm is heated and equipped with a large woodstove, rest rooms, and showers; access to a nearby cookhouse is also available and included in the $9.00 per-person, per-night cost. Reservations are taken starting each October 1 for the following year; interested groups are advised to get their request in early, because popular dates (especially winter weekends after Christmas) fill up fast. For reservations or more information about Harriman State Park, call (208) 558–7368 or write Harriman State Park, HC 66 Box 500, Island Park 83429.

From Island Park, it's possible to take back roads to the last area of Eastern Idaho on our itinerary: the opal mines of Clark County. A2, a county road, runs from just north of Island Park west to Kilgore and on to Spencer, which also site on Interstate 15. ◆ **Spencer Opal Mine** was discovered in 1948 by two deer hunters, and a mining claim was filed in 1952. The Mark L. Stetler family acquired the land in 1964, opened it for digging in 1968, and continue to own and operate the mines today. It's the only place in North America where opals are abundant enough to mine commercially.

The opals rest in layers at the mine, and visitors dig in windrows of opal-bearing rock ranging in size from gravel to small boulders. The mine recommends the following tools be taken to the site: rock hammer, three- or four-pound crack hammer, points and chisels, eight- or 10-pound sledge hammer, bucket, spray bottle, gloves, sturdy shoes or boots, and safety glasses (which are required). Bring drinking water and a lunch, too; water to wash the mined rock is available on site.

If you're interested in digging, stop by the mine's headquarters at the north end of Spencer's Main Street to ask for directions. (There are several mine offices in town; you want the one that's open to the public. It's located at the gas station and trailer court.) The headquarters is open from 7:30 A.M. to 8:00 P.M. except Wednesdays, but digging is permitted only from 8:30 A.M. to 4:00 P.M. Saturdays and Sundays from Memorial Day Weekend through mid-September, with permits issued on site. The cost is $20 per digger per day for up to five pounds of opal-bearing rock; extra pounds cost $3.50 apiece. The mine headquarters also has opal-cutting supplies, rough opal, and finished jewelry, along with a stockpile of rock from the mine for people who don't want to dig. For more information call (208) 374–5476, or write Spencer Opal Mines, HCR 62, Box 2060, Dubois 83423.

# CENTRAL IDAHO MOUNTAINS

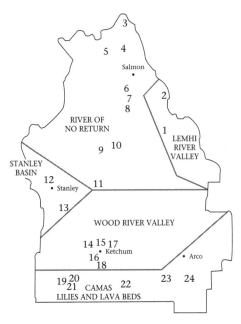

1. Gilmore
2. Lemhi Pass
3. Lost Trail Powder Mountain
4. North Fork Cafe
5. Salmon River Lodge
6. Williams Lake Resort
7. Twin Peaks Ranch
8. Dugout Ranch
9. Challis Hot Springs
10. Custer Motorway
11. Torrey's Burnt Creek Inn
12. Sawtooth Hotel
13. Idaho Rocky Mountain Ranch

14. A Winter's Feast
15. Sun Valley Ice Show
16. Venture Outdoors
17. Hemingway Memorial
18. Povey Pensione
19. Iron Mountain Inn
20. Camas Prairie Bakery
21. Hidden Paradise
22. Silver Creek
23. Craters of the Moon National Monument
24. Big Southern Butte

# CENTRAL IDAHO MOUNTAINS
## LEMHI RIVER VALLEY

When people think of Idaho, they think of mountains, wildlife, and white water. For many residents and visitors, Central Idaho—blessed with all these natural treasures and more—is the region that most epitomizes the Gem State.

Few highways traverse Central Idaho; those that do are separated by mountain ranges. We'll explore this region in a counterclockwise fashion, starting on State Highway 28, the **Sacagawea Memorial Highway.** It is so named because the Lemhi River Valley, which Highway 28 parallels from the town of Leadore north to Salmon, was the birthplace of one of America's greatest heroines, Sacagawea. This Shoshone Indian woman was an invaluable asset to the Lewis and Clark Expedition nearly two centuries ago, as we shall see.

Central Idaho was the site of a major mining boom in the late nineteenth and early twentieth centuries, and the near ghost town of ◆**Gilmore** stands in mute testimony to those days. To get there watch for the historical marker telling of Gilmore near milepost 73, then take the road west immediately across the highway. Gilmore sat about a mile and a half west over a gravel, washboarded road, and its two dozen or so remaining buildings come into view almost immediately. ENJOY BUT DO NOT DESTROY, weathered signs warn the visitor. Look for the remnants of an old railroad bed. This was the Gilmore and Pittsburgh Railway—a branch railroad from Montana—which helped Gilmore's mines produce more than $11.5 million in silver and lead before a power plant explosion ended operations in 1929.

A most rewarding side trip is possible from Highway 28 to ◆**Lemhi Pass,** where Meriwether Lewis became the first white American to cross the Continental Divide in August 1805. Traveling ahead of the rest of the Lewis and Clark expedition, Captain Lewis was searching for the Shoshone Indians in hopes they could provide horses to help the Corps of Discovery travel overland. On August 12, Lewis's party moved west into the mountains from what is now Montana's Clark Canyon Reservoir, following what Lewis called a "large and plain Indian road . . . I therefore did not despair of shortly finding a passage over the mountains and of tasting the waters of the great Columbia this evening." Soon after, Lewis and his men reached a stream that he dubbed "the most distant fountain of the mighty Missouri in search of which we have spent so many toilsome days and restless nights." After pausing for a drink from the stream, Lewis and his men continued to the top of the ridge, where Lewis later wrote he saw "immense ranges of high mountains still to the west of us with their tops partially covered with snow." It was a point of reckoning for the expedition. Lewis had crossed the divide, but the sight of those mountains meant there would be no easy passage to the Columbia.

The day after reaching Lemhi Pass, Lewis and his party came upon several Shoshones, who led the whites to their chief, Cameahwait. Lewis convinced the chief to accompany him back over the pass, where Clark and the rest were waiting with their baggage. It was to be a most extraordinary meeting, for it turned out that Cameahwait was the long-lost brother of Sacagawea, the Shoshone woman who—together with her husband Charbonneau and their infant son—had accompanied the Corps of Discovery after their winter stay in the Mandan Villages of North Dakota. Because of this family coincidence, the expedition was able to get the horses it needed.

To visit Lemhi Pass turn east at the small settlement of Tendoy. The steep and winding 13-mile drive to the pass isn't recommended for large RVs or vehicles towing trailers, but most pickup trucks and passenger vehicles in good shape will make it with no problem. (The Montana approach to the pass is much less steep; apparently a busload of Lewis and Clark buffs made it to the top that way.)

Face west at the pass to see the ridge upon ridge of mountains Lewis described. At 7,373 feet, Lemhi Pass is the highest point on the Lewis and Clark Trail and one of the most pristine, too. It's a great place to watch a sunset, and should you decide to stay the night, the small and primitive Sacagawea Memorial Campground is close at hand. Another campground sits 7.5 miles from the summit. Agency Creek, run by the Bureau of Land Management, has a vault toilet and picnic tables.

Before returning to the highway, note the grave of Chief Tendoy, an Indian leader who commanded respect and influence.

The burial site is sacred to Indians, and visitation by the general public is not considered appropriate. The small store at Tendoy sells gas and food; it's another 20 miles north to Salmon, where all services are available.

# RIVER OF NO RETURN

Salmon is one of Idaho's busiest recreation gateways. Many river trips are outfitted here and at neighboring North Fork, as are many treks into the vast Frank Church-River of No Return Wilderness Area. And skiers in the know make tracks north of town to ◆ **Lost Trail Powder Mountain** on the Idaho-Montana border.

Heavenly, the huge resort on the Nevada-California border at Lake Tahoe, claims it's the only bistate ski area in the United States, but someone forgot to tell them about Lost Trail (or Lookout Pass, another fine little ski hill up on the Idaho-Montana border east of Wallace, for that matter). With just eighteen runs, Lost Trail is among Idaho's smaller ski areas, but its fans praise the hill for its good base and consistent snow quality. The cafeteria ladles up standard fare like burgers and chili in a day lodge where it seems everyone knows everyone else. The closest lodging includes a bed and breakfast and cabins a few miles north into Montana. For more information on Lost Trail Powder Mountain, call (406) 821–3211, or write Lost Trail Powder Mountain, P.O. Box 311, Conner, MT 59827.

The ◆ **North Fork Cafe** at the little town of the same name on U.S. Highway 93 is the restaurant of choice among hungry Idaho river runners, anglers, and hunters. Breakfast offerings include eggs topped with homemade chili, plate-size pancakes, and corned beef hash and eggs. At lunchtime guests chow down on a variety of sandwiches. Steaks, fish, chicken, and hickory-smoked barbecued ribs are among the dinner offerings, and don't forget the huckleberry pie—it's among the best in the state. The North Fork Cafe is open from 6:30 A.M. to 10:00 P.M. in the summer and 7:00 A.M. to 8:00 P.M. daily except Tuesdays during the winter. The phone number is (208) 865–2412.

Head west from North Fork to visit Shoup, which until just a few years ago had the last hand-cranked telephone system in the United

States. West of town on the river at Corn Creek, ◆**Salmon River Lodge** is rock-throwing distance from the Frank Church-River of No Return Wilderness boundary. This picturesque place offers everything from drop-in meals to guided hunting, floating, fishing, and pack trips. Guests enjoy private quarters and bathrooms in a dormitory-style facility, and three home-style meals are served each day. Rates for room and board are about $80 a day, with family and multiday discounts available. If you're just stopping in for a meal, ring the lodge on the old crank phone across the river, and they'll send the jet boat over to pick you up. For lodging reservations or more information, call (800) 635–4717, or write Salmon River Lodge, P.O. Box 927, Salmon 83467.

August is a good time to be in Salmon itself, for that's when the **Great Salmon Valley BalloonFest** takes flight. This event typically features about thirty hot-air balloons from all over the West in races, just-for-fun flying, and the ever-popular night glow. Tethered balloon rides for kids, an arts and crafts fair, a white-water float, a Dutch oven tailgate brunch, and lots of entertainment are among the other attractions. For more information or this year's dates, call the Salmon Valley Chamber of Commerce at (208) 756–2100.

Five miles south of Salmon on U.S. Highway 93, a sign points west to ◆**Williams Lake Resort.** Williams Lake, approached via a mountainous 10-mile road, is a little-known Idaho gem. Cradled in a 5,300-foot valley in the Salmon River Mountains, the lake has lots of rainbow trout and fresh-water shrimp. In addition to fishing, the area boasts a few good trails that circle the lake or climb to a view of the Salmon River Valley.

Williams Lake Resort, on the lake's east side, has boats ready for rent, along with cabins and motel rooms priced from $36 to $115. RV hookups are available, too. The Red Dog Saloon features live entertainment every Friday and Saturday night during the summer, and a restaurant serves good meals from 8:00 A.M. to 10:00 P.M. Try the prime rib at dinner or a stack of pancakes for breakfast. Meal prices are just a bit on the steep side, but the resort sometimes offers some real lodging bargains come fall. For more information call (208) 756–2007, or write Williams Lake Resort, P.O. Box 1150, Salmon 83467.

Fourteen miles south of the Williams Lake turnoff, the traveler

**Williams Lake Resort**

is presented with two more lodging options that couldn't be more different. After crossing the Salmon River, you'll find Twin Peaks Ranch to the north and the legendary Dugout Ranch to the south.

Riding, rafting, and relaxing are the three R's at ❖ **Twin Peaks Ranch,** one of America's oldest dude ranches. Guests who have never been on horseback can learn to ride in the rodeo arena before setting off on gentle trails, while more experienced equestrians have the option of riding high into the Idaho Rockies. Several stocked ponds provide challenge to anglers, and guided trips are offered to seldom-fished private streams. Twin Peaks also offers scenic and white-water floats on the Salmon River, as well as guided hunts for elk and deer.

At Twin Peaks the look is rustic, but creature comforts abound. Three newer cabins have their own Jacuzzi tubs, and an outdoor heated pool and hot tub sit within view of the mountains. Evenings are filled with country line-dance lessons, Western entertainment, and campfires. Dining is Western buffet style, featuring steak or fish, fresh bread and pastries, and Dutch oven desserts. Weather permitting, many of the meals are cooked and served outdoors. Twin Peaks caters to one-week stays, with a per person price of $1,060 to $1,385 for adults and kids age eleven and up. (Children ten and under stay for $850 to $1,100 per week.) Weekly stays in the off-season are discounted 10 percent, and nightly rates are available during May and October at a cost of $170 to $200. No pets are allowed. Call (800) 659–4899 or (208) 894–2290 for reservations or more information, or write Twin Peaks Ranch, P.O. Box 774, Salmon 83467.

The ❖ **Dugout Ranch,** meanwhile, is the homestead of Richard "Dugout Dick" Zimmerman. Dugout Dick has been on this piece of land since 1948, and he says he helped put in the road and the bridge over the Salmon River. But it wasn't until 1969 he started digging caves and multiroom tunnels out of the hillside. He now has about a dozen, and yes, they are available for rent at a cost of $10.00 to $35.00 a month or $2.00 a night. Rooms are outfitted with a woodstove and a bed, although visitors should bring their own sleeping bags.

Dugout Dick's accommodations are certainly spartan, but a handful of people—including a couple from Idaho Falls and a teacher from Missoula—find the caves so cozy they consistently spend their weekends at the Dugout Ranch. One of Idaho's true characters, Dugout Dick has been featured on National Public Radio, in *National Geographic,* and in several books. He'll be glad to tell you a few tales, too. If you stop by the ranch and find it deserted, don't worry—Dick is probably just out on his grocery run to Salmon. Have a look around, and he'll be back before you know it.

Highways 93 and 75 from Salmon to Stanley make up what is perhaps Idaho's best scenic drive. This is the **Salmon River Scenic Byway,** and it can take a while to negotiate. Aside from the road's many twists and turns, many natural roadside attractions vie for the traveler's attention, from the salmon spawning beds to trout fishing near the old Sunbeam Dam, the only dam ever built on the Salmon River.

◆ **Challis Hot Springs,** situated on the Salmon River at the end of Challis Hot Springs Road, was once a boardinghouse for workers from the Yankee Fork, Beardsley, and Custer mines. The springs are now the focus of a year-round RV park and recreational site featuring swimming, soaking, and fishing. The springs site has been in owner Bob Hammond's family for four generations. Some bed-and-breakfast accommodations are available, too. For more information call (208) 879–4442. The address is Challis Hot Springs, HC 63 Box 1779, Challis 83226.

Challis is the jumping-off spot for an optional side trip, the ◆ **Custer Motorway** (alternatively known as Forest Road 070). If you want to take this road, start at the Land of the Yankee Fork Interpretive Center in Challis, then drive the backcountry route 35 miles past panoramic views, old cemeteries, and the 988-ton Yankee Fork Gold Dredge, which searched the river's gravel bars for gold until the mid-1950s. Guided tours are available in the Custer area each summer. From Custer it's just a few miles to Sunbeam and Highway 75, and from there sightseers can head west to Stanley or east back to Challis. Call Land of the Yankee Fork State Park at (208) 879–5244 for more information.

If you need a break from the scenery along the Salmon River or a place to stop for the night, try ◆ **Torrey's Burnt Creek Inn** along Highway 75 west of Clayton. Torrey's was founded in 1923 by Clyde Torrey as a trading post for miners, and it's now best known as one of the main float-trip take-outs along the Salmon.

But the inn may soon be just as famous for its food: People drive from all over Central Idaho to sample Chef Brett Andersen's creative touch with steaks, lobster, shark, salmon, gourmet salads, homemade breads, and more. Torrey's serves lunch and dinner from 11:00 A.M. to 9:00 P.M. daily except Mondays. Reservations are requested but not required; call (208) 838–2313.

Torrey's also has eight authentic log cabins built back in the 1940s when a sawmill was operating on nearby Slate Creek. The ambience is definitely rustic, but the conveniences—microwaves, slow-cookers, and showers—are decidedly modern. The cabins rent for $36 to $65 a night. Call the number above or write Torrey's Burnt Creek Inn, HC 67 Box 725, Clayton 83227-9801.

For many folks a trip to Central Idaho means a float down the Salmon River. Quite a few excursions leave from Sunbeam Village, including those offered by **White Otter Outdoor Adventures.** Whether you want lots of white-water rapids or a calm scenic float, the Salmon delivers. Fun-seekers have their choice of oar boats, where the guide does all the work; paddle rafts, in which floaters help propel the boat downriver; and one-person inflatable kayaks that can be maneuvered by just about anyone fourteen or older. Cost for a half-day float with snack is $50 per teen or adult and $40 for kids; full-day trips including a deluxe meal run $70 for adults and teens, $60 for the small fry. Children must be at least four years old—eight in high-water season—to go floating. Call (208) 726–4331 for reservations or more information.

Some accessible Idaho hot springs are located along Highway 75 west of Sunbeam. East to west there's the very visible **Sunbeam Hot Springs,** complete with bathhouse; **Basin Creek Hot Spring,** located near a campground of the same name; **Campground Hot Spring,** actually located in the Basin Creek Campground (walk into the bushes at site four); **Mormon Bend Hot Spring,** good for late-summer soaking (since a river crossing is necessary); and **Elkhorn Hot Spring.** Although these springs are all located near the highway, soakers are apt to feel a million miles away as they lean back and gaze at the blue sky above.

## THE STANLEY BASIN

If the Tetons are the West's most magnificent mountain range,

Idaho's Sawtooths run a close second. Stanley, situated at the Highway 75-Highway 21 intersection, is the hub of Sawtooth country. In summer there's camping, fishing, and boating on the Salmon River and at Redfish Lake, and there are hikes high into the mountains and adjacent wilderness areas. But for many people winter is prime time in the Stanley Basin because that's when snowmobiling season starts. The area has more than 200 miles of groomed trails and outfitters poised to help visitors with everything from snow machine rental to lodging and meals. For example, **Sawtooth Rentals** charges $100 to $140 per day for a snowmobile; groups of ten people or more get a guide at no extra charge, and snowsuits, boots, helmets, and gloves are available for rent, too. The company also offers package deals with **Creek Side Lodge** in Stanley. These start at about $180 per person and include room, meals, and snowmobile rental. For more information call (208) 774–3409 or (208) 734–4060.

The ✦**Sawtooth Hotel** has been welcoming guests to Stanley since 1931. Hotel guests sleep in handmade, lodgepole pine beds; bathrooms are down the hall. The hotel rooms cost less than $30, double occupancy, but modern motel rooms with private bathrooms also are available for about $45 a night for two. A lobby offers travelers the chance to meet and mingle with fellow vagabonds, read a book, play a game, or have a snack. A restaurant on the premises serves up breakfasts of sourdough pancakes, French toast, and Sawtooth Eggs—one scrambled egg with ham and cheese on toast—along with a good variety of sandwiches for lunch. Guests who will be out for the day can order a picnic or box lunch. In addition to the Sawtooth Hotel, the Cole family operates **Sawtooth Guide Service Inc.,** specializing in fishing trips on the Salmon River. Sawtooth Guides can also set up float trips and spring bear hunts. For more information or room reservations, write the Sawtooth Hotel, P.O. Box 52, Stanley 83278, or call (208) 774–9947.

The ✦**Idaho Rocky Mountain Ranch** south of Stanley ranks among the Gem State's most renowned guest ranches. Built in the 1930s' the ranch offers plenty of activities, although it sometimes seems guests are happiest just relaxing on the huge front porch of the central lodge, with its view of the Sawtooth Mountains. Other on-site diversions include a hot springs swimming pool, horseback riding, horseshoes, volleyball, fishing, and wildlife viewing. Hiking, mountain biking, rafting, and rock climbing are available nearby as well.

Idaho Rocky Mountain Ranch has nine log cabins and four lodge rooms, all with private baths. Breakfast and dinner are served daily, with four or five entrées featured nightly—a typical selection might include fresh Idaho trout, steaks, lamb, and pasta, along with homemade breads and desserts. Summer rates start at $58 per person per night for bed and breakfast or $73 per person per night for breakfast, dinner, and lodging. Both options include the use of all ranch facilities. In winter the cabins remain open for bed-and-breakfast accommodations. Guests can cross-country ski or soak in the hot-water pool while keeping an eye out for the thirty or so elk wintering in the area. Two-night-minimum stays are the rule in winter, with the one-bedroom Homestead Cabin renting for $105 per night, double occupancy. The three-bedroom Winter Cabin (which can sleep up to six people) goes for $125 per night for two, with additional guests costing $15 each per night up to a maximum of four extra people. The cabins are outfitted with an oven, refrigerator, coffeemaker, stereo, towels, linens, dishes, and cookware. For more information or reservations, call (208) 774–3544, or write Idaho Rocky Mountain Ranch, HC 64, Box 9934, Stanley 83278.

Stop at the **Galena Summit overlook** for another great view of the Sawtooth Mountains and the headwaters of the Salmon River. It's hard to believe this tiny trickle of a stream becomes the raging River of No Return, the longest river flowing within one state in the continental United States. Some of Idaho's best tele-mark skiing can be found on the Stanley Basin (or Humble Pie) side of Galena. Gentler terrain is available in the vicinity of **Galena Lodge,** situated at the base of the mountain on the Sun Valley side. The lodge, reopened in 1994 under new management, features hearty food along with ski rentals, lessons, and overnight ski-hut accommodations. From Galena Summit, it's about a half-hour drive to the Sun Valley-Ketchum area.

## WOOD RIVER VALLEY

The Wood River Valley is more famously known as Sun Valley-Ketchum, site of America's first destination ski resort. The skiing is the big draw here, of course, but there are other reasons to visit, too.

Eating is another favorite pastime in the Wood River Valley;

without a doubt, the area is home to some of the state's best and most creative restaurants. But not all fine dining is done indoors. ◆A **Winter's Feast,** based in Ketchum, offers five-course gourmet dinners served by candlelight in an authentic Mongolian-style yurt. The experience is offered nightly December through April, with one seating per evening at 6:15 P.M. Guests arrive at the yurt either by sleigh ride or under their own power on cross-country skis.

Colleen Crain, chef and owner of A Winter's Feast, usually develops several menus each season. A typical repast might include minipizzas topped with home-smoked salmon; garlic soup with Gruyère cheese puffs; romaine salad with honeyed walnuts and bleu cheese; rosemary-roasted rack of lamb with sage potatoes and butternut squash puree as the main course; and, for dessert, a dried-cherry semolina cake with sauce Sabayon. The cost is $55 per person, plus gratuity. Homemade breads, coffee, tea, and hot apple cider are provided, but wine is extra. Reservations should be made at least two days in advance by calling (208) 726–5775.

In the summertime Sun Valley offers a wide selection of special events, but probably none so unique as the ◆**Sun Valley Ice Show.** The biggest stars in figure skating—Katarina Witt, Nancy Kerrigan, Brian Boitano, and Kristi Yamaguchi to name a few—regularly appear on each season's schedule. General admission tickets run about $25 for adults and $20 for children under age thirteen; dinner buffet tickets also are available. Contact the Sun Valley Sports Center at (208) 622–2231 for more information.

Llama trekking is another warm-weather activity growing in popularity in Idaho's mountains. With a sure-footed llama along to carry the load, hikers can wander the state's wild country free of the burden of backpacking. ◆**Venture Outdoors,** a Wood River Valley–based outfitter, offers a variety of llama-supported trips ranging from one-day "Take a Lllama to Lunch" jaunts to multiday educational workshops on such topics as outdoor photography, birds of prey, and wild, edible, and medicinal plants. Trips begin and end in Sun Valley and include transportation, camping gear, licensed guides, and most meals. Cost runs from about $65 per person for a one-day trip to $625 for the five-day Ross Fork Trek. Call (800) 528–LAMA for information, or write Venture Outdoors, P.O. Box 2251, Hailey 83333.

Ernest Hemingway spent part of his last years in Ketchum, and fans of his writing will find several local spots worth a stop. First there's the ◆**Hemingway Memorial** located along Trail Creek east of town; take Sun Valley Road east from the stoplight in downtown Ketchum, and watch for the sign on your right. A short path leads to a memorial as spare as Papa's prose, topped by a rugged bust of the author and embellished by this passage Hemingway wrote in 1939 while in Idaho:

> *Best of all he loved the fall*
> *the leaves yellow on the cottonwoods*
> *leaves floating on the trout streams*
> *and above the hills*
> *the high blue windless skies*
> *. . . now he will be part of them forever.*

Hemingway first came to Idaho in 1939 and visited many times over the next two decades. In 1959 he finally bought a home in Ketchum, but by 1961, apparently depressed over his failing health, he was dead, the victim of a self-inflicted shotgun blast. He is buried in the Ketchum Cemetery, located just north of the downtown area. Look for two pine trees growing closely together near the rear of the graveyard; there you'll find the plots of Ernest Miller Hemingway and his last wife, Mary. Like Jim Morrison's grave in Paris, Hemingway's burial site sometimes attracts people who want to spend some time with the writer's spirit. On one visit this author had been preceded by a pilgrim who had left behind a pack of Dutch Masters little cigars—three left out of the box as if in homage—and an empty bottle of Maker's Mark Whisky.

Hailey and Bellevue, the two "lower valley" towns, are much less known than Ketchum and Sun Valley. That's not saying they lack in glitz, however: actors Bruce Willis and Demi Moore, who live nearby part-time, have been seen bowling at the Mountain Sun Lanes in Bellevue. (Willis is also the man behind The Mint, a formerly working-class bar that has recently undergone an upscale transformation.)

Two blocks west of the stoplight on Hailey's Main Street, the ◆**Povey Pensione** offers four bed-and-breakfast rooms with shared bath. The inn is run by Sam and Terrie Davis, who rebuilt from the ground up a home originally constructed by John Povey, a carpenter from Liverpool, England. A full, hot breakfast is served each morning, with fresh fruit and muffins typically accompanying an egg casserole, French toast, or apple-stuffed German pancakes. Rates at Povey Pensione are $55 for two people, which includes breakfast. The inn is considered unsuitable for children under twelve, and smoking is permitted outdoors only. For reservations call (208) 788–4682 or write Povey Pensione, P.O. Box 1134, Hailey 83333.

## CAMAS LILIES AND LAVA BEDS

South of Bellevue more vehicles topped with ski racks travel the intersection of Idaho Highway 75 and U.S. Highway 20 than any other in Idaho. To the west is Fairfield, another small ski town. The hill here, **Soldier Mountain,** is especially popular with families. Soldier was recently purchased in part by the same couple who run the ◆**Iron Mountain Inn** at 325 West Highway 20 in Fairfield. Named for a fire lookout on the westernmost peak of the Soldier Mountain Range, the restaurant specializes in charbroiled steaks. Come hungry for the prime rib, served Friday and Saturday nights for $9.99. The Iron Mountain Inn is open seven days a week for lunch, dinner, or drinks from 11:00 A.M. to 11:00 P.M. The phone number is (208) 764–2577.

This part of Central Idaho is known as the Camas Prairie for the beautiful blue flowers that were such an important food source for the Indians. (Yes, part of North Central Idaho near the Nez Perce reservation is known as the Camas Prairie, too.) The week before Memorial Day is generally the best time to see the flowers in midbloom; they're at their best the spring after a wet winter. The Camas Prairie is also recognized for its flour, used in the baked goods at the aforementioned Iron Mountain Inn as well as at the ◆**Camas Prairie Bakery.** This little spot in Fairfield's small downtown serves breakfast and lunch from 5:00 A.M. to 3:00 P.M. Monday through Friday. It's also the only espresso place in Camas County—heck, the only one between Mountain Home and the Wood River Valley. The deli-style sandwiches and soups are delicious, and if you're really living right, perhaps you'll arrive on a day Cindee Weatherly has baked one of her three-inch-thick, double-deep-dish pies. If not maybe Cindee—who co-owns the bakery with her husband, Ernie—will make you a pie by special order. Call (208) 764–2100.

Fairfield is also home to ◆**Hidden Paradise,** a particularly apt handle since most Idahoans don't even know it exists. Also known as Soldier Mountain Ranch, the resort offers golf, tennis, and horseback riding in the summer and skiing and snowmobiling come winter. Couples seeking a romantic weekend should ask about the honeymoon suite, featuring a fireplace, sunken tub with mirrors all around it, and a European-style tiled bathroom boasting an oversized shower with two showerheads. The resort also has nineteen log cabins that sleep six to eight people and a lodge suited to parties for up to seventy-five guests. Call (208) 764–2506 for more information or reservations.

East of the Highway 75/20 junction, the traveler soon spies ❖ **Silver Creek,** a fly-fishing dream stream. This was Hemingway's favorite fishing hole, and avid anglers say it's one of the best anywhere, period. Silver Creek runs close to the little ranching town of Picabo, which some lexicologists say is Indian for "silver water." If the town's name—pronounced like the children's game—sounds familiar, it's probably because Picabo's namesake is Picabo Street, the vivacious young skier who captured an Olympic silver medal for the United States in the 1994 Winter Games. Picabo actually grew up in another tiny Wood River Valley town, Triumph.

From Native Americans to early white explorers to the Apollo astronauts, people have long been fascinated with the strange landscape at ❖ **Craters of the Moon National Monument.** Indians probably never lived on the harsh lava lands, but artifacts found in the area show they visited, probably to hunt and gather tachylite—a kind of basaltic volcanic glass—for arrow points. In the early twentieth century, Boisean Robert Limbert extensively explored the lava flows; it was his work and an article he penned in *National Geographic* that led to Craters of the Moon being named a national monument in 1924. In 1969 a group of Apollo astronauts preparing to go to the moon first visited Craters to get a feel for what the lunar landscape might be like.

The same experiences are available today. Though Craters has a popular 7-mile loop drive offering opportunities for several short hikes, it also has a surprisingly accessible designated wilderness area that receives much less use than the rest of the monument. The best time to visit is in the spring, when delicate wildflowers cover the black rock, or in fall after the often-extreme heat of the desert summer abates. In winter the loop road is closed to vehicular traffic but may be enjoyed by cross-country skiers.

There are two predominant types of lava at Craters: the jagged aa (pronounced "ah-ah," Hawaiian for "hard on the feet") and the smoother pahoehoe (also Hawaiian, meaning "ropey" and pronounced "pa-hoy-hoy"). Both may be seen on the North Crater Flow loop trail, a good introduction to the monument's geology. Also consider an overnight stay in Craters's campground; the sites set amid the lava make an absolutely perfect setting for telling ghost stories (although you'll have to do so without a campfire; no wood fires are permitted, since the only available trees are the ancient and slow-growing limber pines). Craters of the Moon National Monument is 18 miles west of Arco. Admission is $4.00 per vehicle (or via a Golden Age, Golden Access, or Golden Eagle passport). For more information call (208) 527–3257.

Craters of the Moon is just a small part of the huge Great Rift section of Idaho, which covers nearly 170,000 acres across the eastern Snake River Plain. For a view of the whole expanse, try a hike or drive up ❖ **Big Southern Butte,** the 300,000-year-old monolith towering 2,500 feet above the surrounding landscape. To get to the butte, follow the signs west from Atomic City. The dirt road up Big Southern Butte is steep, with a 2,000-foot elevation gain and some 15-plus percent grades. It's a challenging hike but one that can be accomplished in a long day's excursion or relatively easy overnight trip. The winds can be fierce atop the butte, but hardy, early-waking campers may be rewarded with a view of the Teton Range against the rising sun.

 **TRAVEL PLANNING RESOURCES**

The following agencies and organizations can provide brochures, maps, and other information about travel in Idaho.

## STATEWIDE TRAVEL INFORMATION:

Idaho Travel Council, 700 West State Street, P.O. Box 83720, Boise 83720-0093. Phone (800) 635–7820.

Idaho Department of Parks and Recreation, Statehouse Mail, Boise 83720. Phone (208) 327–7444.

Bureau of Land Management, 3380 Americana Terrace, Boise 83706. Phone (208) 384–3000.

United States Forest Service, 1750 Front Street, Boise 83702. Phone (208) 364–4100.

Idaho RV Campgrounds Association, P.O. Box 7841, Boise 83707. Phone (800) RV–IDAHO.

## REGIONAL TRAVEL INFORMATION:

North Idaho Travel Committee, P.O. Box 928, Sandpoint 83864. Phone (800) 800–2106.

North Central Idaho Travel Committee, 2207 East Main Street, Suite G, Lewiston 83501. Phone (800) 473–3543.

Southwest Idaho Travel Association, P.O. Box 2106, Boise 83701. Phone (800) 635–5240.

South Central Idaho Travel Committee, 858 Blue Lakes Boulevard North, Twin Falls 83301. Phone (800) 255–8946.

Southeastern Idaho Travel Council, P.O. Box 668, Lava Hot Springs 83246. Phone (800) 423–8597 outside Idaho and (208) 776–5273 inside Idaho.

Yellowstone/Teton Territory (Eastern Idaho), P.O. Box 50498, Idaho Falls 83402. Phone (800) 634–3246 outside Idaho and (208) 523–1010 inside Idaho.

Sun Valley-Ketchum Chamber of Commerce (Central Idaho Mountains), P.O. Box 2420, Sun Valley 83353. Phone (800) 634–3347.

## OTHER HELPFUL PHONE NUMBERS:

General tourism information: (800) VISIT–ID
Statewide winter road report: (208) 336–6600
Forest fire/road closure information: (800) 70–IDAHO
Idaho Outfitters and Guides Association: (208) 342–1919
Idaho Department of Fish and Game: (800) 635–7820
Forest Service camping reservations: (800) 280–CAMP

# INDEX

Entries for Bed and Breakfasts, Inns, Guest Ranches and Resorts, and Restaurants and Cafes appear only in the special indexes on pages 143–44

## BED AND BREAKFASTS AND INNS

## GUEST RANCHES AND RESORTS

## RESTAURANTS AND CAFES

## ABOUT THE AUTHOR

An avid traveler, Julie Fanselow lives and writes in Twin Falls, Idaho. Her previous books include *The Traveler's Guide to the Oregon Trail* and *The Traveler's Guide to the Lewis and Clark Trail*. She edits a features magazine for South Central Idaho, teaches writing at the College of Southern Idaho, and has published articles and essays in numerous national and regional publications including *Trailer Life, Motorland*, the *Wall Street Journal, Entertainment Weekly, Seattle Weekly*, and the *Chicago Tribune*.